OLD PARISH CEMETERY
of NORWOOD,
MASSACHUSETTS

OLD PARISH CEMETERY *of* NORWOOD, MASSACHUSETTS

PATRICIA J. FANNING

THE
History
PRESS

Published by The History Press
Charleston, SC
www.historypress.com

Front cover, left to right: This is the gravestone tympanum of Sarah White, wife of Benjamin White, who died in 1786 at sixty-eight years old. Two obelisks in Old Parish Cemetery with the town hall tower visible in the distance. This unique double tympanum tops the memorial to Ebenezer Everett, a deacon of the South Parish Church, and his wife, Joanna. *OPPV Collection.*
Back cover: The Old Parish Cemetery on a moonlit night. *OPPV Collection.*

First published 2023

Manufactured in the United States

ISBN 9781467154208

Library of Congress Control Number: 2023937169

For all the dedicated members of the Old Parish Preservation Volunteers who have worked to restore and preserve the cemetery.

CONTENTS

FOREWORD

Cemeteries occupy an interesting place in the American psyche. In pop culture, they are the sites for stories of all manner of macabre undertaking; in the lives of many, they are places of profound sadness and other emotions as the final resting place of loved ones; and yet, for some, they are no more than peaceful sites for a walk or run with some of the best landscaping anywhere in a community. Some find cemeteries desirable to live near; others would not reside next to a cemetery if the home was free. Cemeteries range in size and scale from a small churchyard to a small city and are owned by all manner of organizations—from governments large and small to nonprofits, trusts, churches and for-profit corporations.

Old Parish Cemetery in Norwood, Massachusetts, is older than the town *and* the country where it occupies a small hill. The history of Old Parish actually tells *two* stories. One is the story of all those laid to rest there— their lives, their impact on this community and the country, their loves and heartaches, successes, failures, triumphs and tragedies, a veritable history of the human experience, right up until the end.

But there is a second story that has been brought to life by the work of the Old Parish Preservation Volunteers and Norwood's Cemetery Department. When you look at the history of the cemetery itself, you can see the history of this nation and the Town of Norwood. The original site was selected out of necessity; hills yielded little in the way of buildable or plowable land. As time passed, the cemetery's fortunes seemed to ebb and flow with the community and the country, experiencing the same periods of boom and bust. In the mid-twentieth century, the cemetery, eventually ringed by a rusted barbed wire–topped chain link fence, became a forgotten nuisance, a hotspot of teenage shenanigans, underage drinking and even tragedy. But with the start of the restoration efforts in the twenty-first century, the cemetery began to transform into an oasis of calm and serenity in a busy and bustling suburb. Indeed, the history of the last few years of Old Parish breathes more life— no pun intended—into the cemetery than that of its first century.

Today, Old Parish hosts community events, civic gatherings and artistic performances. Despite being two and a half centuries old and not holding a burial in decades, Old Parish is as *alive* as it has ever been. It still chronicles the life and times of the town that surrounds it; the human experience continues to play out on a small hill at the center of a vibrant community.

Tony Mazzucco
General Manager
Town of Norwood

ACKNOWLEDGEMENTS

This book is part of the continuing effort of the Old Parish Preservation Volunteers Inc. to document and disseminate information about the Old Parish Cemetery in Norwood, Massachusetts. It is our mission to preserve and promote this invaluable historical and cultural resource. Thus, the volunteers who stepped up to work in the Old Parish Cemetery are particularly deserving of my gratitude. They have supported the idea of the cemetery's preservation from the beginning, and although they are too numerous to mention, each share in our communal success. I am grateful to Norwood's general manager, Tony Mazzucco; director of Public Works/ town engineer, Mark Ryan; cemetery foremen, Paul Ranalli and Charlie Walsh. I am also thankful for their staff members Tim Fairweather, Fred Hixson, Dan Jones, Mike Reynolds and Tony Scavotto for their support and work in Old Parish. Special thanks to Kate Allendorf, John Grove, Tom Lambert and Leslie Powers, who have given generously of their time with Old Parish Preservation Volunteers Inc. I want to express my gratitude to John and Sue Anderson of the Walpole Historical Society, George Curtis of the Norwood Historical Society, Mary Ann Violette of the First Congregational Church and Vesna Maneva of Halvorson | Tighe and Bond, who provided material or permissions for this book. John Grove also contributed invaluable photography, technological expertise and feedback. I thank Karla Daddieco and Charles Fanning for reading portions of the manuscript. And finally, thanks to my editor Mike Kinsella and the staff at The History Press for their support.

1

ORIGINS

By 1736, when Reverend Thomas Balch was called to the newly sanctioned Second or South Parish of the Church of Christ in Dedham, Massachusetts, the previous incorporation of towns such as Medfield, Bellingham, Wrentham, Needham and Walpole had drastically reduced the geographic area of the community. Still, its population was around 1,200, with less than 100 scattered across the approximately ten square miles that would eventually become the town of Norwood.

The residents who had settled in South Dedham Village, nicknamed Tiot—thought to be a Native word for a land mass surrounded by waterways, which the area certainly was—submitted their first petition for a separate parish district to the general court in Boston in 1717. Although that request, along with subsequent pleas, was denied, the villagers, whom local historian Win Everett characterized as "crabbed, selfish, shrewd, inhospitable farmers" of "straight, pig-headed British descent," persisted.[1] While continuing to pay ministerial taxes to Christ Church in Dedham as required, they began to hold their own religious services in private homes as early as 1722. Finally, in 1728, officials agreed to the request, and two years later, the general court made the establishment of a new parish official.

Only twenty-five years of age and fresh from Cambridge Latin School and Harvard College, the Charlestown-born Thomas Balch accepted the call to South Dedham and was ordained as pastor on June 20, 1736. He married Mary Sumner of Roxbury in 1737, and together, they settled in Tiot for life.

A few years later, with an emerging sense of independence from their mother town, Balch and his congregants desired their own burial ground, something that would allow villagers to be interred within the parish rather than five miles away in Dedham center. For this purpose, parishioner Ebenezer Woodward offered a seemingly useless three-quarters of an acre of steep, uneven land referred to as Sandy Hill to the church free of charge. It stood at the northern end of the village, a little less than a mile from the South Parish meetinghouse. Woodward's proposal was accepted, the graveyard was established and parishioners began to carry their dead along a path that later was well worn and known as Cemetery Street (now Central Street) to be interred on the hill overlooking the village.

The earliest gravestone that is still standing there is one memorializing Azubah Gay. Born on May 31 and christened on June 4, 1738, the child was only three years old when she died on December 3, 1741, the year the graveyard was founded. Her stone reads:

> *AZUBAH GAY*
> *DAU.ʳ TO M.ʳ*
> *TIMOTHY &*
> *M.ʳˢ AZUBAH*
> *GAY AGED 3*
> *YEARS 6 MO 3 D.*
> *DIED DEC.ʳ YE 3.ᵈ*
> *1741*

Azubah was the daughter of Timothy Gay and his wife Azubah Thorp Gay, who had been married on February 10, 1727, and had ten children. As was common in the eighteenth century, several of the couple's children died at a young age. Seth Gay, little Azubah's brother, was buried next to her (he was nine years old when he died in 1753), and her mother and father, who died in 1773 and 1793, respectively, were buried nearby.

Reverend Balch carefully recorded the death of each person, yet there are many who have no corresponding stone in the graveyard. Some continued to inter their deceased family members in Dedham proper; other stones have been lost to time, neglect and weather. But as time passed, the burial place began to fill at the rate of two or three interments a year. In 1751, John Everett, the first deacon of the small parish, was laid to rest.

Born on June 9, 1676, in Dedham, Everett was a well-respected resident of Tiot Village in 1730, when he was authorized to call the first meeting of

The 1741 gravestone of Azubah Gay is the oldest in the cemetery. *Old Parish Preservation Volunteers (OPPV) Collection.*

the South Precinct (soon to be the South Parish) of Dedham. A year later, he was again selected to address the General Court and petition to allow a meetinghouse to be built in the precinct. Upon the organization of the church and the calling of Reverend Thomas Balch to be pastor, Everett was elected the first deacon. He was described by early historian Francis O. Tinker as "an active, intelligent, and pious man, laboring for the good of all."[2] John Everett died on March 29, 1751, at seventy-five years of age.

Nine years later, in 1760, a second of Balch's original deacons, Ezra Morse, passed away. Morse had been an important man in the village, not only as a leader of the church but as a millowner and one of the first to arrive (as a child) in this outpost on the far edge of Dedham. In fact, when the adjacent town of Walpole was incorporated in 1724, Morse's property and mill were situated on the northern border of that community. Like nearly all colonists, Morse served in the militia when called upon and rose to the rank of captain. Ezra Morse even served as a selectman and town clerk in Walpole before petitioning the legislature in Boston in 1738 to have the town lines redrawn so that his land might once again be part of the southern district of Dedham, where he had become a founding member and deacon of the South Parish.

The grave of another, who, as a young man, was among the original fifteen members of the Second Parish, also stands at the crest of the burial ground's highest hill. William Bacon, who was only forty-five when he died, was, in many respects, the quintessential colonist and citizen. Born in 1716, Bacon married Abigail Dean, the daughter of John Dean, another early village settler, when William was twenty-one and Abigail was eighteen. Together, they had eleven children born every few years between 1738 and 1761, the year of Bacon's death. A successful farmer, Bacon owned considerable property (stretching from today's corner of Walpole and Winter Streets to Nichols Street) close to Balch's parsonage. He sold that acreage and moved to an even larger parcel of land at the northern end of the village, bordering West Dedham.

Like most settlers of the mid-eighteenth century, William Bacon was a loyal member of the king's militia; as such, he rose to the rank of captain. In 1755 and 1756, he led a company of men from surrounding towns to Crown Point, New York, during the legendary French and Indian Wars. For the most part, these "wars" were occasional skirmishes separated by long months of inactivity, during which many militiamen may have drunk heavily, broken ranks and even returned to their homes. Thus, in contrast to the British regulars who served for years, most colonists were called upon for intervals lasting only weeks or a few months at a time, enabling them to maintain their livelihoods. Bacon's company served for thirteen weeks in 1755, returning to their homes in December that year. They mustered again in May 1756 and marched from Dedham to Albany across rugged, unsettled western Massachusetts and New York Territory to Fort William Henry at the edge of Lake George.

Bacon kept a diary of the expedition, in which he recounted the court-martial and lashing of one drunken militiaman and the unsanitary camp conditions that led to a multitude of illnesses among his men. After several encounters with the French and their Native allies and suffering the effects of snow in October, the much-diminished Bacon and his cadre of men turned back for Massachusetts in mid-November. He lost six men in battle and about a dozen to disease, both at Lake George and en route home. Marching about ten miles each day, the company found food and lodging where they could; several men were left behind when struck down by sickness. Even after the men were back home, camp-contracted typhoid, dysentery and smallpox continued to arise, resulting in more deaths. When Captain William Bacon died nearly five years later, on May 21, 1761, his death was recorded as being caused by the lingering effects of war.

Two years later, Bacon's widow, Abigail, married George Talbot. Talbot had been widowed twice before and had four children of his own. Abigail and George had one child together, a son, who was born in 1765; George Talbot died on May 24, 1772. The twice-widowed Abigail Dean Bacon Talbot passed away in 1786. Abigail, her two husbands and two of her children with William Bacon were buried side by side in Old Parish Cemetery. Daniel Bacon was two years old at the time of his death in 1750; Hannah was twenty-seven when she passed away on October 15, 1777.

Abigail's gravestone is unusual in two ways. First, her name is misspelled—Tolbard rather than Talbot—and the names of both of her husbands are included on the stone's transcription panel:

In Memory of Mrs.
Abigail Tolbard
(wd. Of Mr. George Tolbard & formerly
ye wife of Cap't William Bacon)
who Died Oct. ye 5th
1786
in ye 67th year
of her
Age.

Still, the stones marking the burial places of Captain William Bacon and Abigail Bacon are two of the most handsome in the graveyard.

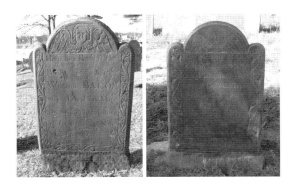

William and Abigail Bacon were well known in eighteenth-century South Dedham. His stone was carved by George Allen Jr. *OPPV Collection.*

The loss of one of Captain Bacon's men during the Crown Point Expedition struck Tiot particularly hard. Thomas Balch, the son and namesake of Reverend Balch, was eighteen when he died of disease in Albany as the company was marching back to Dedham. Bacon sent a sergeant into Albany to retrieve young Balch's belongings, but his pack and money could not be found. Reverend Balch understood the hardships and dangers of military service. In 1745, during King George's War, he had accompanied His Majesty's militia at the Siege of Louisburg on the Isle of Cape Breton in Nova Scotia, Canada. Balch and eight of his comrades, five of whom lost their lives during that mission, were memorialized with a commemorative stone that was erected in 1903 during Norwood's Old Home Day celebration; the stone still stands in Guild Square Park.

The youngest child of Mary and Thomas Balch, born in 1761, five years after the first Thomas's death, was also named Thomas; this second child named Thomas died during the Revolutionary War. The pastor's only other son, Benjamin, born in 1743, attended Harvard and, like his father, became a minister. He served as a chaplain during the Revolutionary War, and afterward, he eventually settled in Barrington, New Hampshire, where he, too, was greatly respected and beloved by his congregation. Three of Balch's daughters married clergymen. Lucy became the wife of Reverend Moses Everett, the grandson of Deacon John Everett and the son of Ebenezer Everett who was also chosen to serve as a deacon of the South Parish's church in 1760. Moses Everett became the ninth minister of Dorchester.

Thomas Balch's daughter Mary wed Reverend Manasseh Cutler, a man of intense intellect and talent who, as chronicled by historian David McCullough in *The Pioneers*, sought to open the Northwest Territory to settlers. Balch's third daughter, Hannah, became the wife of Reverend Jabez Chickering, who had succeeded Balch as minister to the South Parish. Another daughter, Irene, married a Dr. Elijah Hewins from Sharon. Finally, Balch's daughter Elizabeth taught school for a time and then married fellow villager Jonathan Dean. She and Hannah are the only Balch children interred in Old Parish.

It was with much affection and lamentation that Reverend Thomas Balch was laid to rest in January 1774 at the pinnacle of the graveyard that stood within the parish he had led for almost forty years. His widow, referred to as Madam Balch due to her high social standing in the village, an honorific title even engraved on her tombstone, was buried beside him. During his pastorate, Balch had seen his congregation grow from fifteen to approximately two hundred. And he had baptized over six hundred

Reverend Thomas Balch was the first minister called to Dedham's South Parish in 1736. He served for thirty-eight years. *OPPV Collection.*

worshippers and performed close to 150 marriages. One of Norwood's first elementary schools was named after him. Still legible, his stone reads:

> *The Reverend*
> *THOMAS BALCH.*
> *(the first minister in*
> *this place)*
> *died Jan. 8th*
> *1774. In the 63d Year*
> *of his age & the 38th*
> *of his ministry.*

The following year, the village of South Dedham, along with much of eastern Massachusetts, was struck by an epidemic of smallpox. Virulent, contagious and painful with a high mortality rate, the disease was a constant threat in the colonial era. In late 1774, isolated cases began to appear in Boston and the surrounding towns, and the disease continued its relentless spread the next year. After the events of April 1775, the city itself was under British occupation, but that political circumstance did not prevent the virus from escaping into adjacent towns, villages and outlying settlements. The outbreak became so severe that George Washington quarantined his troops and refused to allow anyone from Boston to enter his army's encampment. By then, however, smallpox had reached Tiot with devasting consequences.

In 1775, the population of South Dedham was around 450, and records indicate that from 1765 to 1774, between 6 and 7 residents passed away each year. In the five months between August and December 1775, however, approximately 24 residents died, 16 of them children. Several homesteads, including those of the Morse, Ellis, Fairbanks and Kingsbury families, suffered the loss of more than 1 child. Although some colonists still escorted their dead to Dedham's already ancient graveyard several miles to the north, at least 11 were interred in the South Parish, almost four times the customary number of annual burials. More than seven decades passed before so many were buried in Old Parish in one year again.

For the final quarter of the eighteenth century and the early part of the nineteenth century, the Second Parish was under the spiritual care of Reverend Jabez Chickering. Chickering was born in the part of Dedham that is now Dover in 1753. His father died when he was less than one year old, but his mother taught him the holy scriptures and to honor his father's devotion to God. Perhaps as a consequence, Jabez was a pious child. As legend has it, one day when he was six years old, he was found in his room on his knees, praying. After he graduated from Harvard College in 1774, he accepted the call to the Second Parish of the Church of Christ in Dedham and was ordained at South Dedham on July 3, 1776. He served the parish until his death in 1812. On April 22, 1777, Reverend Chickering married Hannah Balch, the twenty-two-year-old daughter of his predecessor at the church; together, they raised a family in Tiot.

During Reverend Chickering's ministry, 78 parishioners joined the congregation, 203 couples were married and 351 were baptized. The church building itself was the second meetinghouse built by the congregation. It had been erected while the church was still under Reverend Balch's pastorate in 1769 and stood on Lenox Street next to a structure called the Noon House. This edifice had been built as a place for parishioners to gather for meals between the often day-long Sunday services. Chickering's parsonage remained the same two-story residence with a gambrel roof, extended rear ell and welcoming central entrance that had been built for Reverend Balch. The large, well-proportioned house stood about a mile from the new meetinghouse.

According to contemporary accounts, Chickering was an energetic man who gave prudent advice. He was a good scholar in college, liberal in his opinions and wholeheartedly dedicated to God. Sensitive to minor misunderstandings and unkindness, he was forgiving and hospitable and had many warm, lifelong friendships. Especially fond of children, Chickering welcomed them into his services, engaged with them while making his parish visits and always carried treats in his pockets to delight them. For some years before his death, he spent most of his salary on charities, including a fund that was used to support vocal instruction for his congregants that they might sing well during public worship services. Around 1800, he made his collection of books available to his parishioners as a circulating library, an endeavor that lasted a decade or more. It was the beginning of what would later become a secular public library in the community.

Reverend Chickering was an invalid for almost nine months before his death on March 12, 1812, in his fifty-ninth year. His widow, Hannah Balch

These tombs belonged to the Morse, Guild, Chickering and Kingsbury families. The plaque on Reverend Jabez Chickering's tomb was installed in 1961. *OPPV Collection.*

Chickering, continued to reside in the village until her own death in 1839 at the age of eighty-four. The Chickering crypt, one of four on the western side of the burial ground, is constructed of Dedham granite, a local stone with a distinctive pink hue. A plaque was affixed to Chickering's tomb in 1961 by the First Congregational Church (the eventual successor to the Second Parish of the Church of Christ).

During Reverend Chickering's pastorate, certainly one of the most memorable and tragic events that occurred was the sudden death of Captain William Everett in the spring of 1802. Born in the village in 1757, Everett had risen to become a captain in the militia during the uneasy peace that held after the War of Independence. In that role, he played an important part each year in the ceremonial Muster Day, an occasion for militiamen— both former and current—to assemble, parade and run through drills in front of their families, friends and neighbors. According to local historian Win Everett's account, May 4, 1802, dawned brightly in South Dedham. No matter the weather, Muster Day was a holiday in the village. Families from far-flung, isolated homesteads gathered to share food and enjoy camaraderie while exuberant children scurried about, playing games. Watching the militia drills was the central entertainment of the day. Unfortunately, a great deal of drinking took place on Muster Day as well. Both rum and hard cider were available at local taverns, beginning at daybreak.

Unaware that a tragedy was about to occur, the crowd gathered early at the muster field, located on the open, flat plain in the southern part of the village (today, the Balch School stands on the spot). Soon, former soldiers and volunteer militiamen arrived. Most wore their well-worn and now ill-fitting uniforms, some from the Revolutionary War, and carried their equally well-used weapons. When the appointed time came for the official maneuvers to begin, officers called for their troops to assemble. As Captain William Everett waited to give the command that would start the drills, there was a sudden, loud *BANG*! A musket had accidentally gone off, and Captain Everett fell, mortally wounded, on the muster field. The man who shot his musket was reportedly named Morse, but which member of the large Morse family this was remains unclear. It certainly must have been a shock to the good people of Tiot.

Although Win Everett's colorful details might be hyperbolic, there is no doubt that the parish record states: "May 4, 1802, Capt. William Everett, shot dead when exercising his company." And the epitaph on Everett's gravestone confirms the event:

In memory of
Capt. William Everett,
who was kild at the head
of his Company on 4th
May 1802 aged 45 years.

As a tribute to Everett's character, it continues:

Stop, traveler, don't heedless pass him by,
But drop the expressive tear and have a sigh.
Here lies a man whose heart was kind and free.
Whose soul over flowed with Godlike charity.

Perhaps adding to the tragedy, only three months earlier, Everett's wife, the former Sarah Blackman of Stoughton, had died. They left behind nine children between the ages of one and seventeen. After giving her name, date of death, age and relation to Captain William Everett, Sarah's epitaph concludes with the lines:

Stop here, my friend, and shed a tear,
Think of the dust that slumbers here,
And when you read this fate of me,
Think on the glass that runs for thee.

While Sarah Everett's epitaph may seem a cautionary one, a few other stones in the graveyard bear even more ominous messages. Including commemorative inscriptions on tombstones is a centuries-old tradition. Some are descriptors of the person in life (as William Everett's is), others are aphorisms or quotations from holy texts. Some are humorous, and others provide warnings to readers about their own mortality and impending death (as Sarah Everett's does). During the first quarter of the nineteenth century, it seemed the Everett family was particularly prone to offering final words to visitors. The tombstones of Betsey and Joel Everett, the children of Sarah and William, were engraved with distinctive inscriptions as well. Betsey, who died in 1812 at the age of twenty-four, left words of reassurance:

My work was short, I sweetly rest,
God took me home when He saw best.
I am not lost, I shall arrive,
When Christ descends on lower skies.

Betsey's brother, Joel Everett, who died at twenty-five in 1810, left a sterner message:

> *Young men while in your greatest strength*
> *Think not yourself secure,*
> *But be prepared while you have'st health*
> *To meet a dying hour.*

In addition, the stonecutter of Joel's memorial, thought to be carver Coomer Soule II, left a price etched into the lower left corner of the slate: $9.73.

Two other stones that stand not far from those of the Everett family bear similarly engraved prices. The markers of Simon Gould and his wife, Hannah Sumner Gould, were also carved by Coomer Soule II. The descendent of a family of stonecutters who did most of their work in the Worcester area, Coomer labored in shops in Quincy, Canton and Stoughton in the early decades of the nineteenth century. Many of his stones from this period can be found in Canton, Stoughton, Sharon and Norwood. The slate gravestones of Simon Gould, who, like John Everett and Ezra Morse, was

Distinctive because of its epitaph and engraved price, the Joel Everett stone was fashioned in 1810. *OPPV Collection.*

a deacon of the South Parish, and his wife, Hannah, are decorated with a simple motif of urns and willows. Each is marked "$8.00" at its base. Perhaps Joel Everett's more elaborate and lengthier epitaph, which would have taken much longer to engrave, was the reason his stone cost more.

Coomer Soule II also carved the stone that stands above the grave of another early settler of South Dedham. Eliphalet Fisher was born in 1747, a decade after Thomas Balch arrived in the village. His parents, Benjamin and Sarah Fisher, were subsistence farmers, like many who resided in Tiot. Eliphalet Fisher was a member of the local militia and served in the Revolutionary War. On December 5, 1771, Fisher married Judith Bullard, the daughter of Joshua and Ann Bullard. The couple had five children: Eliphalet, Judith, Olive, Obed and Abigail. After Judith died in 1796, Fisher married Relief Blake from Dorchester. Eliphalet and Relief had one child, a daughter, born in 1802. Eliphalet Fisher died in 1819 at the age of seventy-two; his simple tombstone, decorated with a funerary urn and willow branch, is without an elaborate verse or price.

By the 1820s, Tiot was fairly well established, and several developments had lessened its isolation. Although the first stagecoach route through South Dedham (along the Old Post Road, the current Pleasant Street) had allowed for travel between Boston and Bristol, Rhode Island, by 1729, a straighter and less hazardous road was created in 1751. Dubbed the Wrentham Road (present-day Washington and Walpole Streets) because it passed through Dedham to Wrentham and beyond, it carried a regular stagecoach between Boston and Providence. Thus, a stage headed south from Boston would pass the graveyard and the village center once per week. This enabled the eventual development of a business district, starting with a tavern and mailstop. The small cluster of commercial shops was nicknamed "the Hook," after the iron hook on which coaches and travelers tethered their horses. Eventually, villagers no longer had to travel several miles to Dedham for needed supplies and retail goods.

But it was the completion of the Norfolk and Bristol Turnpike, between 1802 and 1806, that changed everything. One of a network of privately built and owned toll roads, this turnpike, for the first time, connected many of the commercial centers of the original thirteen states with each other. When the Norfolk and Bristol (today's Washington Street) was opened, the quiet, self-contained village ceased to be. Trade with the wider world began in earnest.

By 1825, with more than five hundred residents living in South Dedham, the parish felt the need to expand. After lengthy discussions and a rather contentious vote, the old meetinghouse was taken down, and a third, larger

A view of the cemetery from east to west. The sloping terrain is visible. *Courtesy of Halvorson | Tighe and Bond Studio.*

building was constructed on the turnpike. Perhaps as an indication of its significance to the growth of the village, this new two-story church was expected to serve the congregation well into the nineteenth century. At the same time, parishioners began to discuss the need to expand the burial ground. Two years later, with funds raised by individual subscriptions among the congregation, fellow parishioners Lewis Rhoads and his wife, Hannah Ellis Rhoads, were paid forty dollars for more than an acre of land for the purpose of enlarging the burial ground. The graveyard now comprised over two acres bisected by Cemetery Street. The land available for future burial lots gradually sloped away on both sides of Sandy Hill's highest point, from which the oldest tombstones stood watch.

2

DUTY-BOUND

Any visitor to older burial grounds across Massachusetts and New England will find scattered among the oldest graves our nation's first veterans. Some, like those who served in the colonial wars, were British citizens called out to protect not just their own homes but, in many instances, the vast holdings of their king. Ezra Morse, William Bacon and Reverend Thomas Balch were among them. But by 1775, circumstances had changed.

Although the hardy, determined men and women of South Dedham remained His Majesty's subjects, they were third- and fourth-generation New Englanders who had never set foot in the British Isles. Still, they were tied to Great Britain through trade and traditions, language and heredity. They had adhered to rules set forth by royal governors and had paid duties and taxes as prescribed. And yet, with each new generation, the ties that bound these colonists to their sovereign were loosened.

The character of these people—practical, moral, brave and plain-spoken—was shaped by New England and the communities (like Tiot Village) and institutions (like the South Parish Church) they had managed to carve out of the wilderness. Those living in small towns throughout Massachusetts were fatalistic but proud, egalitarian and wary of pretension. And they were growing dissatisfied. They chafed under the Sugar Act of 1764 and, a year later, were indignant at the Stamp Act. It was at this point that an inn at the northern edge of the village became the meeting place of the Dedham branch of the Sons of Liberty, the clandestine association of citizens planning a revolution. Tiot witnessed—and perhaps a few residents participated in—the political actions and sometimes violent resistance that culminated most notably in the Boston Massacre of 1770 and the Boston Tea Party in 1773. While the village and surrounding towns avoided notoriety, like-minded rebellious militiamen had begun to gather and drill. And when the alarm sounded on April 19, 1775, they responded.

More than sixty men, whose ages ranged from fifteen to sixty-nine, left their homes and headed to Dedham center, where they mustered on the common and prepared to join the conflict. Some were able to fire on the British troops as they retreated back to Boston. No less than twenty of these men are interred in Old Parish, including Abel Everett, Jeremiah Kingsbury and Benjamin Lewis. Each man had his own story to tell.

Abel Everett was fifteen years old when he answered the alarm and joined the company of volunteers who mustered in Dedham under the command of Captain William Bullard on April 19, 1775. At that time, Everett had served for twelve days. On January 26, 1776, he was called up for seventeen days for duty at Dorchester during the siege of Boston. Eventually, Everett rose to the rank of captain. He married Mary Smith in 1779 and fathered ten children. His first son died in infancy. A second tragedy occurred on February 20, 1791, when his daughter Lucy, less than two years old, was accidentally scalded to death. Mary Smith Everett died in March 1801. Four months later, Abel Everett married Abigail Guild of Weston.

A few years later, Everett opened a public house on the newly opened Norfolk and Bristol Turnpike. There were few public buildings where either a local resident or a traveler might stop between the Hook and East Walpole. In those early days, the turnpike ran through chiefly wide-open land, with only isolated farmhouses and crop fields on either side. Abigail and Abel Everett had three sons: Horace, Cyrus and Abel. A decade or so following Everett's death on April 2, 1813, his widow, Abigail, sold the land to the parish.

Born on January 9, 1730, in Stoughton, Jeremiah Kingsbury married Abigail Fisher. Two of their children, Abigail and Moses, died during the smallpox epidemic of 1775, just months after Kingsbury, a sergeant in the militia, had taken up arms. Although the records of schools in South Dedham during this period are incomplete, it appears that Jeremiah Kingsbury was the village schoolmaster in the early 1770s, just before the war. Dedham selectmen had approved and constructed a one-story schoolhouse in 1740, enabling the youngsters of Tiot to receive at least some rudimentary education without traveling to Dedham center. At that point, school sessions lasted only a few weeks each year; it was not until

An early schoolmaster, Jeremiah Kingsbury, lost two children in the 1775 smallpox outbreak. *OPPV Collection.*

1760 that both summer and winter sessions began to take place. The first schoolmasters, who had been sent from Dedham, were mostly Ivy League–educated men. None (including Manasseh Cutler) remained in the rural village for long. Subsequently, local men, like Kingsbury, took on the task. Classes continued throughout the Revolutionary War, although the names of these instructors are lost to time. As for Jeremiah Kingsbury, he returned to the village, where he died on June 3, 1788, at the age of fifty-seven. His widow, Abigail, survived him by two decades.

Benjamin Lewis was the youngest of twelve children. In 1765, when he was twenty-five, Benjamin married Hannah Gould of Stoughton, with Reverend Thomas Balch conducting the ceremony. Benjamin and Hannah had six children, all boys. Called up on April 19, 1775, Private Benjamin Lewis spent ten days on duty in Captain Bullard's company. He was later promoted to corporal and, beginning in October 1775, was encamped during the siege of Boston. Benjamin Lewis died in November 1789, knowing he had helped to secure his country's independence.

Once the Revolutionary War had commenced in earnest, more than 120 Tiot farmers, tanners, blacksmiths and others—from a village of forty-three houses and 450 inhabitants—joined the rebellion. After the skirmish at Lexington and Concord and the Battle of Bunker Hill (actually Breed's Hill) in June, British troops settled in Boston, where they awaited reinforcements while colonial troops encircled the city. It was left to George Washington to break the stalemate. An outright attack was not feasible; the cost to his forces would have been far too great. In addition, weary colonial troops were without barracks or firewood and yearned to go home for the winter. Of the eleven regiments that had been recruited (10,000 men), fewer than 1,000 men had agreed to stay. The situation grew ever more complicated: there was no money to pay the men, smallpox continued unabated and a November snow had brought troop morale even lower. As South Dedham's first historian, Francis Tinker observed: "It is hardly possible for us…to conceive of the hardship and sufferings, the Revolutionary fathers were called upon to endure."

Although it was still early in the conflict, both the British command and Washington's war council understood that control of Dorchester Heights could decide the fate of Boston and its harbor, as historian David McCullough discussed in his book *1776*. Yet, neither the British nor Americans dared to move on the Heights before winter. In January, George Washington informed the Continental Congress of the dire circumstances he and his men faced—and his own amazement that the British did not seem to recognize the dolesome condition of his ragtag army. The bitter cold continued through the end of January, barely reaching five degrees Fahrenheit on any given day. Washington wisely waited for the frigid weather to form a pathway strong enough to support troop movements before making the bold decision to take control of Dorchester Heights.

As McCullough tells it, the plan was to occupy the Heights on a single night, before the British could recognize what was happening. Fortifications would be fabricated out of sight; then, with massive manpower and oxen, they would be hauled, along with heavy cannon, up to the summit (much higher and steeper than Breed's Hill). Two thousand Massachusetts militiamen were called out, and work details were dispatched to round up wagons, carts and oxen. Tension mounted throughout the settlements and villages surrounding Boston as the movement of men, equipment and supplies indicated something major was about to take place. But the colonists' success depended on secrecy.

The crucial maneuver began after dark on March 4, 1776, and was completed by the morning of March 5, the anniversary of the Boston Massacre. On the Heights, men toiled steadily with picks and shovels, breaking frozen ground and moving cannons into place all night long. At daybreak, the British were surprised and shocked to see at least twenty cannons and five regiments of riflemen looking down at them. British ships in the harbor sent word that they could not safely remain there unless the rebels were removed from their positions, but the Redcoats' attempt to rally and attack was quashed by a sudden storm of snow, sleet and gale-force winds. Sensing the futility of the action, British general William Howe called off the assault and gave orders to prepare to leave the city. The evacuation of Boston was completed in a matter of weeks. Dorchester Heights was one of the most dramatic and consequential strategic maneuvers of the war. Among those resilient souls who answered the call on March 4, 1776, to aid in the construction of Washington's entrenchments were several men from Tiot. Looking back with awe a century later, Francis Tinker wrote, "When we reflect upon their scanty means, their small numbers, and the greatness of that power they defied, we bow in reverence before their lofty heroism and devotion." Aaron Guild Jr., Oliver Guild, Nathaniel Lewis Jr. and Eliphalet Rhoads each responded to the alarm and joined this perilous mission. Today, the dark-hued slate stones of these men and many others like them can be found on the crest of the cemetery's hill.

Aaron Guild Jr. was born in 1753 and was the first child of Aaron Guild and his wife, Sarah Coney Guild. He joined the Revolutionary War effort at the age of twenty-three and served at Dorchester Heights and elsewhere during the rebellion. Once the war was over, he married Lydia Bacon, the daughter of Captain William and Abigail Dean Bacon (later Talbot), another storied South Dedham family. A farmer like his father, Aaron Guild Jr. died in 1832, having been predeceased by his wife, who passed away in

The oldest stones in the burying ground have stood at the crest of the hill for centuries. *OPPV Collection.*

1794. According to records, their joint gravestone read: "Aaron Guild / died Mar 20, 1832, / aged 79 yrs. / Lydia, his wife, / died May 9, 1794, / aged 36 years." Their tombstone has been lost.

Oliver Guild, born in 1755, was the second son of Aaron Guild and brother to Aaron Guild Jr. According to Revolutionary War records, Oliver Guild answered the alarm on April 19, 1775, although he was only twenty years old. He also saw service in October 1775 and at Dorchester Heights for fourteen days. As the war continued, he was called into service again for twelve months, from January 1778 to January 1779. On July 8, 1779, Oliver Guild married Anna Bullard, who had been born in Dedham as well. Oliver and Anna had four children: Oliver Jr., Salle (who died at three years of age), Lewis and Sally (named for her deceased sister). Oliver died in 1814; Anna Bullard Guild survived him by more than three decades, passing away of old age in 1847.

Nathaniel Lewis Jr. was born in Dedham on July 4, 1731, the son of Nathaniel Lewis and Miriam Draper Lewis. On January 29, 1754, Nathaniel married Experience Hartshorn, who had been born and raised in Boston. Nathaniel and Experience had seven children: Lucy, Nathaniel III, Olive, Rebecca, Jabez, Joseph and Asa. Lucy Lewis died in 1761 at only three years of age. Lewis was over forty when he became one of dozens of South Parish men who responded to the call to arms on April 19, 1775. At that time, he spent ten days on duty in the company of Captain William Bullard. Lewis also served at Dorchester Heights on March 4, 1776. Nathaniel Lewis died "very suddenly" on November 30, 1790, at the age of fifty-nine. Experience Hartshorn Lewis passed away in 1830; her death was attributed to "old age" at ninety-four.

Eliphalet Rhoads was born in 1755. On June 24, 1780, Rhoads married Mercy Holland. The Rhoadses and their descendants remained in South Dedham for generations. Two branches of the family worked in the tanning and the leather industry, leading some of the most successful businesses in the area. Eliphalet Rhoads died on December 2, 1833; his wife, Mercy Holland Rhoads, passed away three years later. During the Revolutionary War, he served for many months with various companies. He was with Captain William Bullard on March 4, 1776, and with Captain Ebenezer Everett in 1778 on an expedition to Rhode Island. Most notably, Rhoads served as a three months man with Captain Aaron Guild at Hull, Massachusetts, beginning in July 1776. In September that year, while still stationed at Hull, Rhoads and others belonging to the battalion petitioned for an increase in pay and for payment of wages, an issue that would become critical after the war. Aaron Guild, a veteran of the colonial wars as well, had a rather illustrious military career and eventually rose to the rank of major.

Born in 1728, a fourth-generation descendant of the first settlers of Dedham, Aaron Guild was a farmer. His homestead stood on Walpole Street, then known as the Wrentham Road; his fields were across the road on land he had purchased from William Bacon. In 1751, Guild married Sarah Coney. The young couple had two children: Aaron Jr. and Oliver. Within two weeks of Oliver's baptism, Sarah died on February 18, 1755, just shy of her twenty-second birthday. Guild married Annah Coney (Sarah's sister) sometime in 1756. Annah Guild kept the farm going while her husband served in the French and Indian War. Together, they had eight children. Annah Coney Guild died in 1776, leaving her husband with the children, whose ages ranged from nineteen-year-old Sarah to Nathaniel, who was barely one. And the Revolutionary War was ongoing.

In December 1777, Aaron Guild was married for the third time. His wife, Sarah Blackman May, was a widow from nearby Stoughton. Aaron and Sarah grew old together. She passed away in 1812, and Major Aaron Guild died on February 3, 1818, having lived through—but not participated in—yet another war with Great Britain.

Although he was one of the dozens of men from Dedham who participated in the American Revolution, Aaron Guild has come to represent colonial heroism and patriotism to the community at large. In 1902, during Norwood's Old Home Day celebration, a monument commemorating his response to the alarm on April 19, 1775, was unveiled in front of the town's library on property he once owned. It reads, "Near this spot / Capt Aaron Guild / On April 19, 1775 / Left plow in furrow, oxen standing / and departing for

Lexington, / arrived in time to fire upon / the retreating British." Of course, Guild, along with his fellow militiamen, actually headed not to Lexington but to Dedham, where they mustered. But in 1902, the sentiment was pure: the town wanted to honor the activities of the Patriots of 1775. At the time the tribute was made, officials stated that Guild was not being honored as an individual but rather "as a type of many who showed their heroic devotion" to the cause of independence.[3] A few years later, the image of Guild leaving his oxen and plow behind was adopted as the town seal. That seemed to codify Guild's place in Norwood history.

Aaron Guild garnered more acclaim when his name was adopted by the local chapter of the Daughters of the American Revolution (DAR) in 1975. Founded in 1890, the DAR was created to memorialize the country's colonial era history. To gain membership in the group, a woman was required to prove lineal descent from a Patriot of the American Revolution. Since its founding, the organization has admitted more than 900,000 members. Today, the DAR has adopted a mission to include preservation, education and community service and has chapters across the United States. In 1983, the Aaron Guild Chapter of the DAR placed a commemorative plaque on Guild's grave. But he was not the only Guild interred in the cemetery to be so honored.

In 2012, the DAR placed a plaque at the grave site of Martha May Guild Kimball, signifying that Martha was a "Real Daughter" of the American Revolution. Born in 1803, Martha Guild was the daughter of Jacob Guild and his wife, Chloe May Guild. Jacob was the son of Aaron Guild and his second wife, Annah Coney Guild. Born in 1760, he was a teenager when the war began but a man by its close. In 1780, he married Chloe May, the daughter of his father's third wife, Sarah. When they married, Jacob was twenty and Chloe was sixteen.

Martha, their youngest child, was well educated for the period. She attended the Sanderson Academy in Ashfield, Massachusetts, where she was a classmate of Mary Lyon, who went on to found Mount Holyoke College. Martha taught in local private schools for almost twenty years before she founded the "Old Frog Pond School" (so named because an underground brook formed a small pond beside the school building) in 1844. It was said she was an excellent teacher and headmistress, attracting the best students from local families for more than a decade. After retiring from teaching, Martha Guild married Caleb Kimball, a minister from Medway. Martha Guild Kimball joined the Daughters of the American Revolution sometime between the group's founding in 1890 and her death in 1898.

These plaques were placed at the graves of Aaron Guild and Martha Guild Kimball by the National Daughters of the American Revolution. *OPPV Collection.*

Because she was both a DAR member and the daughter of a soldier, or Patriot, the organization designated her a "Real Daughter" of the American Revolution. According to the DAR, Martha May Guild Kimball was the only "authentic" Daughter of the American Revolution buried in Norwood, thus the only woman deserving of their unique plaque.

Following the Revolutionary War, the political landscape continued to churn uneasily. The next few decades were rife with poverty, cultural and economic instability and, eventually, more military activity. A monetary crisis contributed to people's anxiety and insecurity. Many army and militia veterans had received little pay for their service during the war. In addition, businessmen and traders, both in Europe and America, who were owed money refused to extend more credit and began to demand cash payments for their transactions. Caught in the middle, countless rural farmers and tradesmen, having no cash and no compensation, lost their livelihoods and property to debt collectors. The resulting economic crisis affected many areas but especially western Massachusetts. In 1786, when the state legislature failed to address the issue, a disgruntled former soldier named Daniel Shays led hundreds of armed men to protest at county courthouses and prevent the execution of foreclosures. As months passed, their tactics escalated toward insurrection.

In response, the governor of the commonwealth dispatched over 1,200 militiamen to oppose Shays. In January 1787, these state-sponsored soldiers faced the rebellious force as they attempted to enter the Springfield,

Massachusetts federal armory in search of weapons. The militia routed Shays and his disorganized band, most of whom fled to Vermont, only to be captured later. Most of these men, including Daniel Shays, subsequently received a general pardon. As a result of this incident, historically known as Shays Rebellion, the Massachusetts legislature ultimately enacted laws to ease the economic crisis.

According to Tiot historian Francis Tinker, no rebellious activity occurred in South Dedham, but twelve men from the village enlisted to protect the government and disperse the insurrectionists. Two of the men sent to put down the rebellion in Springfield are interred in Old Parish: William Everett, who, in 1802, lost his life on Muster Day, and twenty-three-year-old Joel Guild.

Guild, himself a veteran of the Revolutionary War (he joined as a very young man), was another son of Captain Aaron Guild and his second wife, Annah Coney Guild. Two years after the encounter with Shays, he married Hannah Weatherbee, and they had nine children. Guild became the village blacksmith and died on January 14, 1842. His wife, Hannah, died in December that same year.

Volunteers were recruited, outfitted and sent into battle once more at the beginning of the nineteenth century, when the British and Americans renewed hostilities. The War of 1812 finally established the independence of the United States once and for all. From the spring of 1813 until the close of the conflict, British ships hovered along the Atlantic coast and threatened the destruction of maritime cities and towns. Officials anticipated attacks on Boston, which had a large shipbuilding industry and was a city of some wealth. There was actually little fighting along the New England shoreline during the war, but the commonwealth felt the pressure on its industries, the drain on its economy and a general sense of insecurity among its people. Caleb Strong, the governor of Massachusetts at the time, was opposed to the war, as were many successful businessmen, because such a conflict might interfere with the region's shipping interests. It was not until after territory in Maine was lost to the British that the governor took measures to protect the Massachusetts coast. A large number of citizens of all classes and trades volunteered, and a fort was built in East Boston. On September 6, 1814, Strong issued an order for the state militia to be ready to march to Boston on a moment's notice. Most companies of soldiers served in the city from September 10 to October 30 that year. (Essentially concluded on December 24, 1814, the War of 1812 was officially declared at an end on February 18, 1815, by President James Madison.) Joel Talbot and Daniel Hartshorn were among those who enlisted in the conflict.

Joel Talbot, who was born in South Dedham, enlisted as a private in Captain William Davenport's detached company, which was raised in Milton. He was in service at South Boston from September 13 to November 7, 1814. A carpenter by trade, Talbot returned to South Dedham, married Hannah Fuller of the village and had four children: Elizabeth, George, Henry and Joel. Three of their children predeceased their parents. The youngest, Joel F., died in October 1841 of bilious fever at the age of nineteen. (An obsolete term today, bilious fever was usually the diagnosis for any fever accompanied by nausea and diarrhea.) Elizabeth died on January 18, 1850, of tuberculosis at the age of thirty-three (her gravestone, erected at a later date, erroneously gives her birth and death dates as 1826 and 1866). Henry, a cabinetmaker, died on September 18, 1866, of pulmonary tuberculosis. According to cemetery records, he was buried in Brockton, Massachusetts. Hannah Talbot, eighty-six, passed away of old age in October 1877. A few months later, on February 17, 1878, Joel Talbot died at the age of ninety-three. His death, too, was attributed to old age.

The second War of 1812 veteran buried in the cemetery was Daniel Hartshorn, who was born in adjacent Walpole, Massachusetts, on March 13, 1787. In 1802, while Hartshorn was residing there, Walpole formed the Walpole Light Infantry. Proud of the unit, the community outfitted each of the volunteers with a high leather hat with silvered brass mountings and a cockade. Perhaps due to its weight, this elaborate hat was rather quickly

This picturesque view of the graveyard's sloping terrain includes stones from the mid- to late nineteenth century. *Courtesy of Halvorson | Tighe and Bond Studio.*

replaced by a more traditional cap. Likewise, a light, trim rifle was substituted for the initially issued flintlock gun, which was so heavy it required a soldier to rest during firing.

Captain Warren Clapp was in command of the Walpole Light Infantry when the twenty-five-year-old Daniel Hartshorn enlisted as an ensign at the start of the war. Clapp led the unit on its march to Boston and during the time it spent securing the harbor. Ensign Daniel Hartshorn was in service in Boston from September 10, 1814, to October 30, 1814.

By 1831, Daniel and his wife, Polly Ellis Hartshorn, who were married in 1810 and had two sons, had come to the South Parish of Dedham, where he tried his hand at farming. Daniel died in July 1871 at the age of eighty-four. Less than a year later, his widow, Polly, passed away on April 5, 1872, just over a month after South Dedham was incorporated as the town of Norwood.

Because he was not living in the village at the time of his service in the War of 1812, Hartshorn's name was not included on the memorial tablets that hang in Norwood's town hall, but his service should be honored. The graves of Joel Talbot and Daniel Hartshorn stand beside each other on a ridge in the center of the cemetery.

3

ARTISTS IN STONE

Gravestone carving was a craft tradition for centuries, but it remains an overlooked and underappreciated art form. Harriette Merrifield Forbes pioneered the study of early American gravestones in a 1927 essay (reprinted in her 1967 book, *Gravestones of Early New England*). Since then, scholars continue to work and publish in this field. Discovering and exploring networks of cutters, apprentices, their lives and their work, they help tell the stories of gravestone artists whose work can be found in the Old Parish Cemetery.

As one might imagine, not all stones are signed, and many identifying marks are belowground, seen only if the stone is toppled or removed to be reset. Experts in the art often recognize a particular cutter through the characteristics of their work; each carver had their own design preference, ornamentation style and lettering technique. Design elements examined on these early tombstones are the tympanum (central arch); the finial, or shoulder (these can be round or flat); the side border panels; and the central tablet, or transcription panel (where the epitaph is engraved). Material also matters. Cutters worked with both slate and marble. Slate was most often used for colonial-era stones; quarries were plentiful in the New England area. Unpolished marble came into use by the first third of the nineteenth century, and granite became the dominant material later in the century. Since the burial place for the Second Parish of Dedham was founded around 1740, slate was the predominant material for the earliest tombstones.

The art on the stones follows a common pattern as well. In the mid- to late eighteenth century, the fire and brimstone warnings of Calvinist clergy were still prevalent, even in the village of Tiot. (After all, Reverend Balch had been one of a score of Protestant clergymen who traveled with colonial troops to Cape Breton to drive the Jesuits from Louisburg in 1745.) Many local pastors were still preaching the tenets of predestination, eternal damnation and the fear of retribution from a wrathful God. Not surprisingly, gravestones reflected these anxieties. Foreboding and forbidding hourglasses or effigies of winged skulls and crossbones warned of the rapid passage of time and the inevitability of death. The central arches on the stones of Mary Lovett Morse (1746), the wife of Ezra Morse, one of the village's founders, and Benjamin Fairbanks (1757) are examples of these harsh reminders.

These depictions slowly evolved into winged angels and generic faces, images that perhaps encouraged those left behind to consider the promise of redemption and resurrection. The carver George Allen Jr. crafted stones in Old Parish with both kinds of effigies. George Allen Jr. was born in 1742 to George and Sarah Allen of Rehoboth, Massachusetts. His father, George Sr., was a stonecutter, as was his brother Gabriel. Working primarily in the

This early winged skull and crossbones were carved on the gravestone of Mary Morse, the wife of Ezra Morse, who died in 1746. *OPPV Collection.*

Providence, Rhode Island and southeastern Massachusetts area, the family's creativity and unique style influenced many later carvers. George Jr. began carving when he was a teenager, and his skill allowed him to swiftly master various styles. Tragically, he died at the age of twenty-two, leaving only about three dozen stones that can be unquestionably attributed to him.

In Old Parish, Allen's winged skull and cherub work are represented on the stones of Ezra Morse and William Bacon, respectively. His design on Morse's stone, carved in 1760, demonstrates his distinctive round eyes, undercut jaw and double outlining between the skull and wings. Only a year later, he completed the tombstone for William Bacon (see the image on page 17). This decidedly male face with an impish mouth, puffy eyes, straight nose and well-coiffed hair exudes strength rather than doom, and the intricate background detail is characteristic of Allen Jr.'s work as well. Also distinctive are the side border panels of leafy vines suspended from carefully etched rosettes.

Sarah Lewis Morse died in 1767, "very suddenly" after returning home from the Sunday meeting. Although George Allen Jr. died three years before her, a third stone cut by Allen memorializes Sarah, a seeming impossibility explained by the uncertain nature of the stonecutter's craft. Gravestone carving was usually not a full-time occupation, because carvers could not support themselves on the income made from stonecutting alone. For most of the eighteenth and early nineteenth centuries, cutting was an artisanal trade carried out by farmers, blacksmiths and tradesmen as time permitted. Thus, carvers often prepared stones when they had time, leaving the transcription panel to be filled in as the need arose. If the artist passed away, as in this case, the text was engraved by a second carver. Sarah Morse's (1767) stone has the undercut jaw and border vines characteristic of Allen Jr., but according to experts, the lettering was probably done by Daniel Farrington.

Born in Wrentham in 1733, Daniel Farrington was active in Wrentham town business in addition to his work as a stonecutter. At times, he was a fence viewer, a constable, a warden and an assessor for that community. Working out of a shop on South Street (today's Route 1), Farrington developed a sure hand in both design and lettering. Beginning in the 1770s, his mature work displayed squint-eyed, winged and round doll-faced effigies. Often, he cut relief carving on the wing feathers and border rosettes that provided depth and dimension; his later wing feathers have a shirred, bat-wing look. There are more than twenty examples of Farrington's work in Old Parish. Two of his most impressive stones are those of husband and wife David and Anna Fairbanks.

Stonecutter Daniel Farrington of Wrentham created these gravestones for Anna and David Fairbanks. *OPPV Collection.*

David Fairbanks was born in South Dedham in 1731 and married Anna Wight when he was twenty years old. He served in the French and Indian Wars and, nearly a decade later, responded to the Lexington militia alarm in April 1775. In March 1776, he aided in the construction of Washington's fortifications at Dorchester. Thus, like many, he took up arms both for and against the King. Farrington's handsome stone, with its unique wig style, was complemented by its powerful inscription:

> *In memory of Cap.*
> *David Fairbanks,*
> *who Died April 19th*
> *1776*
> *in ye 45th year*
> *of his*
> *Age.*
> *Beneath this stone Death's prisoner lies,*
> *the stone shall move the prisoner rise,*
> *When Jesus with Almighty word*
> *calls his dead saints to meet their Lord.*

Farrington carved an equally affecting round-eyed, doll-like effigy with border panels for Anna Fairbanks, who died nine years after her husband.

He had, by then, apparently become a favorite stonecutter of the Fairbanks family of South Dedham. In addition to the stones of Anna and David, there are more than a dozen other Farrington stones completed for Fairbanks relatives, including the particularly poignant tomb of two sons of Anna and David, both named Lemuel. One died at five years of age in 1761, and the other died at three years of age in 1770.

Farrington was also the artist who carved the remarkable double stone belonging to Ebenezer and Joanna Everett (see the image on cover). Everett, the son of Deacon John Everett, was born in 1707, and he married Joanna Stevens in March 1734. He was chosen as a deacon of the South Parish's church on November 30, 1760, a post he held until his death on May 19, 1778, at the age of seventy-one. Joanna Stevens Everett died on June 21, 1791. Ebenezer and Joanna Everett were the parents of eleven children, including Reverend Moses Everett, the ninth minister of Dorchester who married Reverend Thomas Balch's daughter Lucy, and Rev. Oliver Everett, the fourth pastor of the New South Church in Boston. They were the grandparents of the orator and statesman Governor Edward Everett (the son of Reverend Oliver Everett).

According to historian Vincent Luti, Farrington's mature work remained extremely competent and consistent. For nearly thirty years, he made few changes in style, design or ornamentation, an observation confirmed by his work in this burial place. The artist's distinctive lettering remained stable as well, helping make his work easily identifiable. Daniel Farrington died in Wrentham in September 1807.

Like the winged death's head, the rising sun is a very obvious symbol of resurrection, eternal life and the light of heaven. While the setting sun symbolizes death and the end of one's earthly life, the rising sun evokes the promise of renewed life and the beginning of life after death. In Old Parish Cemetery, there are two gravestones that use the sun as their dominant symbol.

Abigail Millett Ellis, the wife of William Ellis, was born in Gloucester, Massachusetts, in 1696. She married Ellis in 1720, and they had eight children born between 1721 and 1738. Abigail died in 1763, when she was sixty-seven years old. Her gravestone was carved by John New of Wrentham. The eyes of the sun just breaking the horizon, with ornate rays exploding into varied shapes and swirls carved into concentric semicircles on the stone's tympanum, are an example of New's inventive design work. Mary Smith Everett's stone was simpler but striking. Married to Abel Everett in 1779, she gave birth to ten children and died in March 1801. The lettering and design

Decorated with a setting or rising sun, this memorial belongs to Mary Smith Everett, who was forty-one when she died in 1801. *OPPV Collection.*

on Mary's stone by a yet unidentified carver remains sharp and clear despite the two hundred years that have passed. The arch on this stone depicts a well-balanced sun with bright eyes and radiating sunbeams, complemented by well-defined floral side border panels. The dramatic carving of the single word "Sacred" on the first line of the stone's tablet assures the passerby that Mary is confident of her eternal life in heaven. The inscription panel reads: Sacred / To the memory of / MRS. MARY / wife of Mr. Abel Everett. / who died March 17, / 1801. In the 41 year / of her age.

As the eighteenth century came to a close, wings and faces became less common and eventually gave way to more secular designs. Softer imagery began to prevail, inspired by a lessening of the Puritan sensibility surrounding sinfulness and retribution, the notion that worldly success was acceptable and even encouraged, plus a desire to be "modern." Neoclassical symbols, such as funerary urns and weeping willows, became popular in gravestone art. This secularization of the religious consciousness also reflected a cultural shift in focus from the deceased to the mourner. The message etched in stone became less about guilt and judgment and more about the pain of loss.

As the nineteenth century progressed, nearly every aspect of death and burial changed. Marble replaced slate as the favored material for tombstones for a variety of reasons. Marble was easier to quarry and to sculpt, opening up the possibility of elaborate, three-dimensional design elements. (Unfortunately, marble also weathers more rapidly than slate. Today, while much of the lettering and ornamentation on slate stones remains as crisp as the day it was cut, many marble stones are barely legible, their decorations having nearly melted away.) Marble was also a "lighter" material, more closely resembling the white ceramic of the then newly popular household ceramic goods. Even more significant, perhaps, is that while the dark slate was a remnant of the severe beliefs of the past, marble mirrored the more hopeful, uplifting attitudes of "New Light" Christians who embraced a forgiving and kind savior instead of a vengeful and wrathful God. Eventually, marble grave markers became quite plain, with only a name and date carved into the stone. Formal phrasing, such as "Here lies," "In memory of" or even "Sacred to the memory of" were no longer in use. Finally, of course, the word *cemetery* replaced *burial ground* or *graveyard*, words that had come to seem almost medieval. In the Old Parish Cemetery, the next generation of stone carvers, who labored under these transitioning attitudes, are represented by Alpheus Cary and Michael Gallagher.

Alpheus Cary was born in Quincy, Massachusetts, in 1788. As scholar James Blachowicz notes, Cary advertised as a stonecutter in Boston business directories from 1810 until the 1850s (he died in 1869), and he developed a large, upper-class clientele. In 1831, Cary was one of the original proprietors of Mount Auburn Cemetery in Cambridge, which, as the model for the new rural cemetery, prohibited the use of slate markers. Although he has many signed memorials at Mount Auburn, and there are examples of his work in burial places throughout New England, Cary did more than simply carve stones. He was the stone mason for the construction of St. Paul's Church on Tremont Street in Boston, and he supplied the marble tablet for the John and Abigail Adams monument in Quincy's United First Parish Church.

Cary's gravestone designs varied from plain lettering to willow and urn decoration and elaborate scenes on a tombstone's tympanum. Cary set the standard for the modern stonecutter with his unique combination of artistic talent and business acumen. The Alpheus Cary stone in Old Parish Cemetery was identified as it was being repaired and reset by volunteers. It is a simple, elegant stone of marble in a two-way tablet style. Cary's signature was revealed as volunteers lifted the broken bottom section of the stone of Charles T. Pond from the ground.

The simple marble stone of Charles T. Pond, carved by Alpheus Cary, was signed by the artist. *OPPV Collection.*

Charles Thurston Pond was born in neighboring Walpole, Massachusetts. In 1841, he married Martha Sumner, the daughter of Moses Sumner and Catherine Gay Sumner. The Sumner family was well known in South Dedham; Moses was a cabinet maker and the brother of Joseph Sumner, the proprietor of the South Dedham Tavern that stood on the main roadway through the village. Catherine Gay Sumner had spent her early years on a farm on Pleasant Street, the Old Post Road that was the first highway connecting Dedham with the wider world. Martha was the Sumners' first child. She married Pond when she was nineteen, and they had one child, Charles Edwin Pond, born in 1842. Only four years later, Charles Thurston Pond died of a brain disease at the age of twenty-nine. Martha Sumner Pond remarried. Both she and her second husband, Ebenezer Gay, are interred in the Sumner family plot. Charles T. Pond's stone stands alone within the same lot.

Born more than a quarter century after Cary, Michael Gallagher emigrated from County Longford, Ireland, in 1828. He became a United States citizen, married Mary Ann McArdle of Boston and settled in Canton, Massachusetts, a community adjacent to South Dedham, around 1840. According to Canton historian Daniel Huntoon, Gallagher manned the toll gate on what is Route 138 today and learned his trade from a stonemason named Lewis Johnson, who had a workshop nearby. Eventually, Gallagher moved to a house with an adjoining shop on Washington Street in Canton and gained a reputation as a carver. He even built a windmill next to his workshop so that he might split and grind stones more easily.

In 1847, Gallagher advertised his business in the *Norfolk Democrat*, a local newspaper, noting that he completed work "on reasonable terms" and "at short notice." Correspondence found in the Canton Historical Society archives indicates that same year, he traveled to Sing-Sing, New York, to acquire a particular type of stone. He worked in both slate and marble, and in his study of Gallagher's oeuvre, James Blachowicz states the artist carved large, three-dimensional monuments as well. By 1850, Gallagher was apparently successful enough that his household, already consisting of his wife and three children, had expanded to include six young men, possibly his brothers and brothers-in-law, all of whom listed their occupation as "marble cutter." According to Blachowicz, Gallagher produced at least 237 stones between 1833 and 1854. His slate work is identified by funerary urns with a distinctive neck, narrow pedestal and scallops cut into a crest-shaped interior design. Gallagher carved fulsome willows with finely drawn internal branches and leaves.

Perhaps due to the proximity of his shop, there are several Gallagher stones in Tiot's cemetery, including the double stone of Elizabeth and Jonathan Dean. Jonathan Dean was born on August 7, 1730, served in the Revolutionary War and then returned to South Dedham, where he died at the age of seventy-five. His wife, Elizabeth Balch Dean, was the daughter of Reverend Thomas Balch. As noted on the stone, the monument was erected sometime after her death in 1820 and is inscribed:

In memory of Mr. Jonathan Dean
who died Sept. 8, 1805
aged 75 years

In memory of Mrs. Elizabeth,
wife of Mr. Jonathan Dean,
and dau, of Rev. Thomas Balch
who died Sept 15, 1820
aged 74 years

Erected out of filial regard for their memory
by their youngest sons, Ebenezer and Balch Dean.

Michael Gallagher, a stonecutter from Canton, Massachusetts, engraved and signed this memorial to Jonathan and Elizabeth Dean. *OPPV Collection.*

Fully visible on the bottom right corner of the stone is the carver's name, "M. Gallagher, Sc." (Michael Gallagher, sculptor). The tombstones of Elizabeth Bullard, who died in 1841, and Olive Dean Bullard, who died in 1843, bear Gallagher's signature as well.

It was not unusual to have stones erected long after the death of an individual. Unlike the Deans, who appear to have sought this tribute to their mother and father decades after their demise, some families awaited the death of a surviving spouse so that the names of both might be engraved on one memorial tablet together; others may have been delayed by an inability to purchase an appropriate marker. Whatever the reason, such postdating was a common occurrence in nineteenth-century graveyards.

The stone of Samuel Holmes Dean, the son of Elizabeth and Jonathan Dean, is another example of a postdated stone by Michael Gallagher. Born in 1767, Samuel was the Deans' first child; his brothers Ebenezer and Balch commissioned the slate stone for their parents mentioned previously. Samuel Dean married Deborah Lewis in 1789, and the couple had six children. Samuel died in 1827, but it was not until his wife's death twenty years later that matching marble tombstones were placed on their graves. Each is a simple rectangular tablet, and each bears Gallagher's signature.

Although he was a talented carver who took pride in his craft and worked hard to build a business, Michael Gallagher had his personal demons. In

1847, the Gallaghers' first child, six-year-old Michael Thomas Gallagher, died. That same year, Jane Endicott, a neighbor of the stone carver, observed that Gallagher had given up alcohol. In 1851, however, a year in which Gallagher and his wife lost twin sons at birth, Endicott noted that the artisan had relapsed. Shortly afterward, he was involved in an unpleasant incident at a local tavern. Sadly, when he died four years later, his cause of death was listed as intemperance; Michael Gallagher was forty-two years old. He and his son Michael Thomas were buried in the Canton Corner Cemetery, surrounded by many examples of Gallagher's own work.[4]

There are many marble stones in Old Parish Cemetery that were carved by as yet unidentified makers. Some have the elaborate, three-dimensional floral elements that were possible when a craftsman worked in marble. The significance of floral and plant symbolism varied by time, place and belief system. Generally, flowers represented life's beauty and its fleeting nature. Still, each flower or bouquet represented particular ideals and feelings; some even conveyed a characteristic of the deceased. For example, sheaves of wheat represented immortality and resurrection; oak leaves were a symbol of patience, endurance and strength; and ivy generally symbolized friendship— each a common, comforting symbol. On the other hand, the cattail, known by Christians as the reeds among which Moses was found floating in a tiny basket, became a metaphor for the servant of the Lord who lived a life of humble obedience. Thus, a bouquet of cattails was often chosen to grace the stone of a particularly devout person. There are about a dozen unique floral-decorated stones in Old Parish; most have been weather-softened over the years, but their beauty remains.

Most poignant, though, are the smallest stones, shaped like tiny houses or decorated with a lamb, a child's prone figure or a wreath, marking the grave of a child—or sometimes two. One small marble gravestone on the edge of the cemetery is the marker for two young siblings: Samuel and Albert Johnson. Their father, Edward Johnson, was born in England. On November 22, 1870, in Boston, he married Catherine (her name was variously recorded as Katherine, Catharine and Katharine) McCormick; she had been born in Ireland. Sometime in the early 1870s, the couple made their way to South Dedham, where Johnson found work as a laborer. On December 18, 1871, Samuel Johnson was born. He died one day later due to "imperfect development." In 1873, twins Edward William Johnson and Ellen Jane Johnson were born. Three years later, the family welcomed a fourth child, Albert Chandler Johnson. Sadly, Albert died on July 6, 1878, of dysentery. Soon after that, the family moved to Lancaster, Wisconsin,

These two small marble headstones, marking the graves of children, have been cleaned and reset by volunteers. *OPPV Collection*.

where Edward Johnson purchased a farm. He died in 1890 at the age of forty-seven. Catherine and her children remained in Wisconsin, where she passed away in 1913. Over the years, Catherine Johnson likely thought back to a tiny gravestone standing alone in Old Parish Cemetery. The fading inscription on the back of the stone reads: "SAMUEL. / Died Dec. 19, 1871 AE 1 day / ALBERT C. / July 6, 1878 / AE 2 yrs 5 mos. 14 dys / Children of Edward & Catherine Johnson."

Another family named Johnson (not related to Catherine and Edward) had a tragic story as well. George W. Johnson was born in 1801 in Sharon, and he married Nancy Lewis in 1828. The couple settled in Walpole, Massachusetts, where George Johnson became a grocer and postmaster. Sometime around 1843, George and Nancy had a daughter, Julia E. Johnson. In 1865, Julia Johnson married Harlin P. Baker, a house painter. Harlin and Julia had two sons: Harlin William "H. Willie" Baker, born on October 4, 1872, and George Henry Baker, who was born in 1874 and died in infancy. That same year, Julia Johnson Baker's father, George W. Johnson, passed away and was buried in Old Parish Cemetery.

Harlin P. Baker died about a year later. In May 1876, Julia Johnson Baker married Lewis E. Warner. It was the second marriage for each. Julia and Lewis Warner, who was a baggage master on the railroad, resided in Norwood, where their twin sons, Lewis Edward Warner and Edward Lewis Warner, were born on March 3, 1878. A little over two months later, on May 19, 1878, Lewis Edward died of pertussis, also known as whooping cough, a highly contagious disease that was often deadly for children. On January 22, 1879, H. Willie Baker, then six years old, died of scarlet fever. Both boys were buried alongside their grandfather, and a small gravestone bearing their names was erected. Now quite faded from weather, it is inscribed:

H. WILLIE.
DIED JAN. 22,
1879.
AGED 6 YEARS
3 MOS. 18 DAYS
LEWIS E. JR.
DIED MAY 19,
1878.
AGED 2 MOS 21 DAYS
CHILDREN OF
LEWIS E. &
JULIA E. WARNER

By the latter part of the nineteenth century, when these two young families erected memorials to their young boys, the handcrafted work of the stonecutter was being replaced by the less artisanal, more commercial monument manufacturer. These two marble markers, as well as those with floral ornaments, were likely created not by hand, but by machine. Gravestone carving was no different from any other business caught in an ever more urban and industrial landscape. Capitalism, with its dependency on specialization, mechanization and the division of labor, took hold of society. Local tradesmen, who decades earlier may have bartered or extended credit to those in need of their services, were being supplanted by larger companies with owners, workers and a business plan.

One of the first entrepreneurs in the field of stone production was David Allen Burt of Newton, Massachusetts. Born in 1830, Burt apprenticed in Taunton, Massachusetts, with Samuel Warren, and by 1847, he was working with Alpheus Cary, the monumentalist who helped found Mount Auburn

Cemetery. After six years of training, Burt returned to Taunton, bought out the shop of Samuel Warren and opened not simply a workshop but a showroom. Burt quickly made a name for himself, and his business took on the characteristics of a factory. He employed designers, salesmen, marble workers and even teamsters to deliver his gravestones to burial sites. Although the upper classes could obtain the sculpted stone of their choice (the very wealthy had mausoleums built to their own specifications), most customers, with the advice of a salesperson, chose from a preproduced array of model stones. Once the selection was made, all that was needed was the insertion of a name and date. If desired, a few standard phrases of inspirational text or scripture could be ordered as well. James Blachowicz notes that Burt even published a compendium of possible epitaphs divided into categories,

This monumental memorial belonging to a branch of the Morse family is an example of a modern granite gravestone. *OPPV Collection.*

such as adults, soldiers, children and even lines "Appropriate for Catholics." The gravestone had become merchandise.

Burt's business flourished. In 1877, his son David Arthur Burt took over the enterprise; the elder Burt died in 1894. It is difficult to trace all of the company's work, but the impressive granite monument dedicated to a branch of the Morse family that stands near the Washington Street entrance of Old Parish Cemetery bears the signature "Burt and Company, Taunton." With this type of memorial, characterized by polished granite and machine etching, gravestones became even more substantial and seemingly impervious. They no longer bore the marks, mistakes and misspellings of an individual artisan, however. The age of the craftsman had truly ended.

4

CRISES AND CHANGE

series of crises occurred in South Dedham during the mid-nineteenth century. Each had an impact on the cemetery itself. As the village developed, farming—both agricultural and dairy—remained the economic mainstay of the community, but the rise in manufacturing was significant. The tannery, which had been founded by Abner Guild in 1776, and the paper mill, operated by the Ellis family beginning in 1812, each benefited from their proximity to the Wrentham Road. With the opening of the Norfolk and Bristol Turnpike, however, commercial opportunities abounded. The Everett Furniture Factory, situated less than a mile south of the Hook, was one of the first to take advantage of the access to the larger market that the turnpike offered. But it was Moses Guild III who really understood the potential of the new road.

Born on December 8, 1792, Moses Guild III was the son of Moses Guild Jr. and Abigail Everett Guild, both of Dedham. In April 1820, Moses married Julitte Ellis, the daughter of John and Hannah Ellis. They had two children: Moses Ellis Guild and George Dwight Guild. Like his father and grandfather before him, Moses Guild III was a prominent man in South Dedham and became one of the wealthiest men in the village. His grandfather, also named Moses Guild, was a Revolutionary War veteran and the brother of Major Aaron Guild. Recognizing a need, his father, Moses Guild Jr., founded a fleet of freight wagons that ran between Boston and Providence over the Norfolk and Bristol Turnpike. After his father's death in 1829, Moses III continued in the business for another two decades. In addition, he was South Dedham's first postmaster.

Established on December 18, 1846, a year before the first U.S. postage stamps were issued, the post office was an institution in name only; in reality, it was a three-foot-tall cylindrical letter wheel made of wood and tin into which mail was inserted. After closing the freight business, which waned when railroad transport arrived, Guild converted the structure built to house freight wagons and equipment into a playing card factory. Subsequently, the building became a rudimentary tenement for Irish immigrants. Moses Guild III died in April 1857. Julitte Ellis Guild died in April 1872 of pneumonia at the age of eighty, just months after South Dedham was incorporated as the new town of Norwood. Their graves, marked by a plain marble stone, are located on the western side of the cemetery, next to the grave of Guild's father, Moses Guild Jr. Buried alongside them are two of their grandchildren, Moses Dwight Guild and Minnie French Guild, the children of their son Moses Ellis Guild and his wife, Sarah Ann.

As the grave site of the Guilds indicates, by the mid-nineteenth century, the cemetery had turned to face the turnpike, renamed Washington Street in the 1870s. Encircled by a carriage way just wide enough for a horse-drawn hearse, the burial ground's uneven terrain had no footpaths. Like the village center itself, the graveyard had developed in a haphazard, almost casual manner since its founding. A century passed before large plots—on the lower elevations—were laid out and purchased by local families. By that time, the cemetery no longer belonged simply to the parish.

Following the death of Reverend Jabez Chickering, who served thirty-six years as pastor, the congregation of the South Parish chose Reverend William Cogswell to lead them. He began his pastorate in 1815 and remained for fourteen years, during which a number of religious, societal and cultural shifts took place. It began in 1824 with a name change; the Church of Christ in Dedham Second Parish officially became the South Church of Dedham. Two years later, parishioners voted to build a new meetinghouse (the third in the congregation's history) on the east side of the turnpike near the corner of today's Walnut Avenue. Erected on the site of Captain Abel Everett's tavern, the building was known as the "1828 Meeting House." That same year, some thirty-five of the younger parishioners of the South Church—a sizeable percentage of the membership—broke from the orthodox covenant and formed the First Universalist Society of South Dedham.

Founded in 1793 in Oxford, Massachusetts, Universalism embraced the doctrine of universal salvation, that is that no matter how serious one's sins, a reconciliation with God was possible. In addition, Universalism expanded the notion of individual faith to include social responsibility

Volunteers gather to learn
how to clean and reset
the gravestones of Moses
Guild Jr. and his wife,
Abigail Everett Guild.
OPPV Collection.

and strongly advocated for social reforms, such as temperance, women's
rights, prison reform and the abolition of slavery. Since its inception in
1736, the South Church had remained steadfast in the orthodox tenets of
Christ Church of Dedham, doctrines which these younger, more liberal
congregants now considered extreme. They had begun to debate the issue
among themselves in 1827, and shortly thereafter, they incorporated. The
withdrawal of these members from the South Church caused considerable
upheaval and consternation. The rift between the two denominations was
deep, and it tore families apart. It took decades for long-standing and even
familial associations to heal. At the outset, these renegade parishioners
held their services at the South Dedham Tavern, then owned by Joseph
Sumner, a member of the new society.

Born on April 28, 1797, Joseph Sumner was the grandson of Nathanael
Sumner, a deacon of the early South Parish Church. On July 22, 1821,
he married Charlotte Rhoads, the daughter of Eliphalet Rhoads and
Mercy Holland Rhoads. Charlotte Sumner gave birth to a daughter in

1823 and passed away shortly thereafter from postnatal complications, an all-too-common occurrence in the nineteenth century. Joseph Sumner was remarried a few months later to Elizabeth "Betsey" Huntley. That same year, he became the proprietor of the South Dedham Tavern. Located in the village center, the tavern had become a mainstay of village life and the site of what little commerce there was in the town.

In 1829, the Universalists built and dedicated a meetinghouse on property now occupied by St. Catherine's School. In keeping with his support of the sect, Sumner opened a second-floor suite of rooms at his tavern for the home of the society's first pastor. Alfred V. Bassett was a twenty-four-year-old theology student when he answered the call from South Dedham. On December 26, 1831, Reverend Bassett died by suicide in his rooms at the tavern after cutting his throat with a razor. The act shocked and saddened his congregation. Famed Universalist Thomas Whittemore delivered the sermon at Bassett's funeral. Describing the young man as amiable and intelligent but subject to mood swings ranging from exuberance to deep melancholy (likely a then-undiagnosable bipolar condition), Whittemore noted that Bassett was well loved by his family and well respected by his parishioners. He assured the congregation that Bassett was suffering from his illness when he died.

Fifty years later, Reverend Edwin Thompson, who, too, ministered to the Universalist congregation, recounted the events he had witnessed when, as a young teacher in the village, he had been invited by Bassett to share his rooms at the tavern. He considered Bassett pleasant, talented and a good friend. On the day prior to his death, Bassett complained of being feverish but promised he would see a physician if he was not better by morning. That night, Thompson was awakened by an "unearthly groan" and found the body of Bassett. As Thompson summarized it, the death "of course caused much excitement at the time in his parish,

Reverend Alfred V. Bassett, the first Universalist Society pastor, was beloved by his congregation. *OPPV Collection*.

town and the whole vicinity. It was a great public sensation and, as such, was soon over; but the private griefs, the disappointed hopes, the blighted affections of many individuals to whom he was very near and dear, were too deep for all these long years to erase."[5]

Despite the schism between the South Church and the newly founded Universalists (and some South Church parishioners secretly delighting in the tragedy), the young minister was allowed to be interred in the parish burial ground. Bassett was one of the first non–church members to be so permitted. Weathered by time, the stone is barely legible:

To the
Memory
Of
REV. ALFRED V. BASSETT
Pastor of the
Universalist Society
In Dedham
Died Dec. 26, 1831,
Aged 25 years:
He was deeply beloved by
the flock of which he was
pastor and died lamented
by all who knew him.

Edwin Thompson returned to Tiot when, having embraced the Universalist faith in 1833, he was called to the ministry at South Dedham in 1841. Outgoing and extremely popular, Thompson, who was nicknamed "Little Thompson" due to his short stature, became a leader in the Total Abstinence Movement and frowned on the sale of liquor at Joseph Sumner's tavern. When confronted, Sumner offered to stop selling rum if he could find someone to buy up his existing stock. As the story goes, Thompson took him up on the offer, bought the liquor himself and destroyed it. Joseph Sumner remained the proprietor of the (now dry) South Dedham Tavern until he sold it to Richard Hartshorn in the 1850s. Sumner died on September 13, 1877, at the age of eighty. His widow, Betsey, died two years later. Both deaths were recorded as being due to old age.

The next crisis to have an impact on the cemetery was not the result of a religious debate but a natural disaster. In 1849, in yet another transportation advancement, the Norfolk County Railroad Company connected the track systems of the Boston and Providence and the Boston and Worcester railroad lines. The company then extended the line through Dedham, South Dedham and Walpole, all the way to Blackstone, Rhode Island. It was the beginning of an era that featured a host of takeovers and consolidations among several railroad companies and conglomerates. As noted earlier, by the 1840s, the graveyard was spread over several acres of land extending from today's Washington Street to what later became Hill Street; Cemetery Street, the access point for funeral corteges, split the property nearly in two. As the decade came to a close, the Norfolk County Railroad was constructed at the eastern edge of this property.

And then, according to noted local historian Fred Holland Day, disaster struck. While researching Tiot's early settlers and their graveyard, he found that several graves seemed to be missing. Working in the late nineteenth century, Day was able to speak with aged residents and learned that a fairly large portion of the burial ground was washed away by a great storm shortly after the railroad was completed. "There is no record of the many graves so destroyed," according to Day, "but it is certain that no small number disappeared at that time."[6] Some trace of these graves remains, however. Here and there within the cemetery stand rows of tombstones that nearly touch each other. It is probable that these early markers, many of which are damaged, were salvaged from the destruction and reset within familial plots.

Around this time, the South Church installed its sixth pastor, Moses McLellan Colburn, who had been born in Vermont. Colburn graduated from the University of Vermont in 1844 and the Andover Theological Seminary in 1850. He was ordained in New Bedford and was called to the South Church in 1852. In December that same year, Reverend Colburn married Maria A. Read, a Vermont native. The couple had three children, two of whom died in infancy. One son, John David Colburn, who passed away in 1858, was buried in Old Parish Cemetery. In November 1861, Maria Colburn died of tuberculosis at the age of thirty-six and was buried beside her son. In 1863, Reverend Colburn married Harriet E. Read, the sister of his first wife; they remained in South Dedham until 1866. Reverend Colburn died a decade later in Michigan, where he was interred.

Chester and Sarah Comey also suffered the heartbreaking loss of children. Born in 1832 in Foxboro, Massachusetts, Chester Holbrook Comey was educated at Bridgewater Normal School. Comey came to Tiot in 1857 and was the Everett School's schoolmaster from 1857 to 1863. He and his wife, the former Sarah Rich, had four children, only one of whom reached adulthood. Three of their children, Frank Holbrook Comey, Louisa Greenby

A row of tombstones that were likely placed together following the partial destruction of the cemetery by severe storms in the mid-1850s. *OPPV Collection.*

Comey and Phillip Robinson Comey, were buried along with their parents in a large lot facing the carriage way in the cemetery. Chester Comey's stone, which was badly damaged and recently repaired, reads: "Chester H. Comey / Born Feb. 22, 1838 / Died Mar. 31, 1881 / He Doeth All Things Well." Near this marble marker, three small stones were placed, one for each child. The memorials to these children have been reset.

Another man who had an impact on the village was George Hill. Installed as pastor of the Universalist Church (the First Universalist Society became the Universalist Church in 1856) in 1865, Hill served in that capacity for seventeen years. Born in 1825 in Meredith, New Hampshire, where he attended local schools, Hill was ordained a Universalist preacher at the age of twenty-six and held pastorates in Arlington and Milford, Massachusetts, before coming to South Dedham. Only a year earlier, the Universalists had built a new church building near the center of the Hook. Looking back years

Granite coping encircles the family lot that contains the graves of Chester Comey; his wife, Sarah; and their three children. *OPPV Collection.*

later, Hill recalled that when he arrived, there were only about 1,250 residents in Tiot, and yet, the villagers supported four churches, two schoolhouses, two grocery stores, two dry goods stores, a livery stable, a cobbler's shop and a carriage and blacksmith's shop.[7] In addition to his ministerial duties, Hill involved himself in all aspects of the community. He was a leader of the temperance union, one of the organizers of the business association, a member of the board of health and a trustee of the public library.

There is no doubt that George Hill, with his kindness, intelligence and devotion to the entire village, helped to heal the wounds of the acrimonious South Church/Universalist Church split while he conducted funerals for his parishioners in what began to be called the "Old Cemetery." Sadly, Reverend George Hill was also drawn into one of the most notorious events in South Dedham history: the murder-suicide of the Carlos Marston family.

Dr. Carlos Marston, a homeopathic physician, had come to Tiot in the late 1850s. He and his family, which included his wife, Susanna Tenney Marston, and an adopted daughter, Cora T. Harris, had living quarters in the South Dedham Tavern, now owned and operated by Richard Hartshorn. From all reports, Susanna Marston had a long history of experiencing instability and depression. Just prior to the tragic events of September 1, 1865, her behavior had become so erratic that acquaintances began to avoid her. At times, she was seen talking to herself; at other times, she mumbled incoherently and had a distressed look about her. As her condition worsened, a nurse attendant was hired to care for Susanna, but Dr. Marston remained concerned.

Although he had taken up his post in the Universalist Church only earlier that year, Reverend Hill had already become a good friend to the physician; the two men would converse about many things, and Marston had confided in the minister about his worries. It was to counsel his parishioner on that subject that Hill visited Marston's apartment on the evening of August 31, 1865. The preacher and doctor talked well into the night about the situation. Ultimately, Marston decided that no matter how much he dreaded the idea, he had to commit his wife to an insane hospital, a profoundly unpleasant institution in the mid-nineteenth century.

Perhaps Susanna Marston, who was thought to be asleep in her room, overheard the hushed conversation, or perhaps she had been planning her actions for some time. In any event, after Reverend Hill departed, Dr. Marston went to the room of the nurse and told her that both Cora and Mrs. Marston were asleep for the night and that she should retire herself. He suggested she lock her door so that Susanna, who had been especially troublesome that day, would not disturb her during the night. The nurse did as he recommended.

Around four o'clock in the morning, Susanna Marston, who had somehow gained possession of her husband's revolver, slipped from her room and into her husband's chamber and shot the doctor in the head. She then went to her adopted daughter Cora's room, where she shot and killed

The South Dedham Tavern, later called the Norwood House, was the site of major events in the village. *Courtesy of the Morrill Memorial Library.*

the ten-year-old. Finally returning to her own bedroom, she took her own life. A passing milkman, hearing the shots, hurried to awaken tavern owner Dick Hartshorn. Together, they ran upstairs to the doctor's apartment and found the bodies of the deceased. The nurse, still bolted in her room, was unharmed. The constable and Dr. David Fogg, another local physician, were called; both confirmed the horrific events. Officially recorded as a "murder and suicide," it was the first crime of its kind to take place in South Dedham.

The tragedy and all its lurid details were recounted in newspapers, tabloids and gazettes throughout New England and New York, including the *Boston Traveler*, the *New York Herald* and *Frank Leslie's Illustrated Newspaper*. Almost seventy years later, in August 1934, Norwood newspaperman Win Everett wrote about the startling crime and the Marstons' gravestone "leaning stark and alone under a great tree on the hill." The marker still stands there, at the farthest edge of the cemetery, facing the east wind, its back to the rest of the community of stone. Cracked, damaged and toppled, it has been repaired, reset and cleaned. Its words worn almost invisible with time, the stone remains a stark reminder of a tragic event:

> *CARLOS MARSTON, M.D.*
> *Died Sept. 1, 1865*
> *Aged 42 Years*
> *SUSANNA E. TENNEY*
> *Wife of C. Marston*
> *Died Sept. 1, 1865*
> *Aged 36 Years*
> *CORA T. HARRIS*
> *Adopted Daughter of*
> *C. and S.E. Marston*
> *Died Sept. 1, 1865*
> *Aged 10 Years*

During the latter part of the 1860s, discussions about independence from Dedham reached their peak in Tiot. A strong industrial base had helped the village prosper, but resentment over taxation, public works and education had increased. South Dedham residents believed they were not receiving adequate resources or services for the taxes they were contributing to the mother town. People were particularly concerned about the inadequate school facilities and the village's representation at Dedham town meetings. In December 1871, South Dedham residents selected a committee to present

Damaged and weathered, the gravestone of the Dr. Carlos Marston family stands as a reminder of a horrifying crime. *OPPV Collection.*

a petition—signed by over 80 percent of the legal voters of the village—to the state legislature, requesting the area be set off and incorporated as an independent town. The committee was led by Josiah Warren "Shout" Talbot.

Born in 1785 and educated in the Sharon, Massachusetts public schools, Talbot's interests and expertise were wide-ranging. He studied popular sciences, such as phrenology (a theory linking personality traits to head and skull shape) and pomology (apple breeding). After arriving in South Dedham around 1860, he became, in turn, a teacher, minister, orator, apple and grape expert and general horticulturist. At various times, he was also a spring bed manufacturer and a photographer. He acquired the nickname "Shout" after he was struck by lightning as a child and lost his hearing in one ear; people were, thus, required to shout for him to hear them. For all his eccentricities, Talbot was recognized as a respected citizen of the village and leader of the independence movement. Before Talbot's death and interment in the cemetery in 1873, South Dedham had, indeed, become the Town of Norwood.

After initial reservations were resolved, the act of incorporation was approved by the general court and signed by Governor William B. Washburn. When it came to selecting a name for the new town, Reverend George Hill again provided counsel. According to local statesman and scion of the Winslow Brothers tannery Francis O. Winslow, it was Hill who proposed the name "Norwood," perhaps because of his familiarity with the writings of Henry Ward Beecher, who had authored the popular book *Norwood, or Village Life in New England* in 1868. (There is another version of the naming in which Norwood as a name was proposed by Tyler Thayer, a contractor. Thayer supposedly said that the word *Norwood* looked good in print, had no I to dot or T to cross and there was only one other town by that name in the country. The truth of the matter is lost to history.) Either way, the town was separated from Dedham and incorporated as the Town of Norwood on February 23, 1872.

Five years later, in February 1877, another extraordinary set of circumstances occurred, which resulted in a death and burial in the old cemetery: a case of hydrophobia (human rabies). Annie Bragdon, an eighteen-year-old housemaid who worked in Norwood, was bitten between the fore and middle finger of her right hand by a small terrier dog in August 1876. Believing her injury to be slight, Bragdon did not seek medical aid at that time, although the dog was destroyed to satisfy popular superstitions. Annie's broken skin healed rapidly, and she appeared to be in good health. Six months later, however, on February 14, 1877, while washing dishes in warm water, Annie suddenly felt a sharp pain at the site of the bite. As the night progressed, the pain extended up her arm and to her shoulder. The next morning, she had difficulty swallowing and felt a constriction in her neck and upper chest. She consulted Dr. David Fogg of Norwood, the same physician who was called to the Marston apartment. Fogg immediately recognized the symptoms as those of hydrophobia and advised her to return to her home in Hyde Park, where Dr. C.L. Edwards saw her that same evening. Edwards found her calm, with nothing unusual about her appearance. When he offered her some water, however, her throat contracted severely, and spasms ensued. Although the young woman tried to ingest the liquid, she could not. Annie was put to bed and told to remain perfectly quiet.

By 3:00 a.m., Bragdon was suffering from severe muscle contractions, and her skin was moist and hot. She was given a small amount of morphine to quiet her, but she could not sleep. When the doctor returned, even a slight noise would bring on spasms, and swallowing had become extremely painful. With each hour, her condition worsened, and her spasms increased. Finally, she settled down and was relatively calm for about two hours prior to her death, which took place at 9:30 a.m., only sixty-two hours after her symptoms first appeared. Annie Bragdon was buried in Old Parish beside her father, John Bragdon, who had passed away from cancer two years earlier. Her mother, Julia Pomeroy Bragdon, died in 1891 of heart disease. She, too, was interred in the cemetery. No marker was raised above their graves.

Annie Bragdon's tragic death drew unwanted and inaccurate attention from the press. On February 17, 1877, the *Boston Daily Globe* reported that the young woman "was seized with sudden spasm, and jumped from the bed, foaming at the mouth and snapping at all who approached her." The physicians who had attended her, however, denied that account. Nor did she bark like a dog, as was reported elsewhere. Dr. Edwards published the details of the case in the *Boston Medical and Surgical Journal* (the predecessor of today's *New England Journal of Medicine*) and explained that her very harsh, dry cough could have been interpreted as a bark-like sound by an uninformed observer. In 2006, Dr. Philip M. Teigen of the National Library of Medicine in Maryland used the Bragdon episode in his study of a cultural panic caused by a series of human rabies cases in Massachusetts between 1876 and 1881. According to Dr. Teigen, Annie Bragdon's case was "one of the best documented cases, not only in Massachusetts but in all of the United States and Canada."[8]

Sometime in 1884, a severe storm caused considerable damage in Norwood; the bridge on Short Street was washed away, and a large culvert under Washington Street at the northern end of town had to be relaid. There was no mention of the Old Parish Cemetery, but perhaps there was further erosion on the east side of the cemetery's hill. For some reason, in 1885, the town sought permission from the state to lower the grade of the cemetery. On April 1, 1885, the selectmen were authorized "to lower the grade of old parish cemetery…and to remove, replace, and re-inter the remains of the dead and the monuments erected in their memory." The legislature's permission was contingent on the town giving proper notice of the work to interested parties and assurances that the remains and monuments be reinterred and re-erected "in substantially the same relative positions" after the change of grade.[9]

It appears those plans were never carried out, however. Instead, $800 was appropriated the following year to build a retaining wall, likely the granite wall that is still there, leaving the highest hill of the cemetery to continue its slow erosion.

5

ABOLITION AND REBELLION

T he half-decade between 1860 and 1865 proved to be monumental in virtually every township across the nation. In the village of South Dedham, it was no different. Still a community of only 1,250, Tiot responded valiantly when, as Francis Tinker put it rather dramatically in his "History of Norwood," "The cohorts of slavery unfurled the black flag of treason." After President Lincoln declared war on the Confederacy, posters and proclamations calling for volunteers appeared at public buildings around the commonwealth. A verse written by a Tiot poet captured the spirit of the times:

I can't tell what their fate may be,
Nor can the storm allay,
That now doth seem to threaten them
Upon their future way;
I can but hope war's dreadful clouds
Will soon appear from view,
With Union safe, and triumph for,
The Red and White and Blue!

And if the Army triumphs not,
When traitorous hosts appear.
It will not be the fault of a
South Dedham Volunteer;

For we will rally round our flag
In danger's darksome day,
And strive with all our earnestness
To drive the foe away![10]

As they had during past conflicts, South Dedham men chose to serve their nation, and the village quickly surpassed the quota assigned to it. Although they served in several units throughout the war, many enlisted in the Second Massachusetts Volunteers, the Eighteenth Massachusetts Volunteers, the Twenty-Fourth Massachusetts Volunteers and the Forty-Third Massachusetts Volunteers.

South Dedham residents had been well informed of the struggle for abolition by their former Universalist pastor Reverend Edwin Thompson, who had been part of the antislavery movement for nearly thirty years. Thompson was born in 1809 in Lynn, Massachusetts. As a teenager, he took up the abolitionist cause and was active in the Young Men's Anti-Slavery Society of Lynn. By the early 1830s, he was speaking throughout the state, often in the company of abolitionist leaders William Lloyd Garrison, Wendell Phillips and Angelina Grimké. He organized local societies and antislavery libraries in Essex, Plymouth and Bristol Counties. Residing in Walpole, Massachusetts, after taking up the pastorate of South Dedham's Universalist Society in 1841, Thompson wrote vehemently in favor of abolition in the local newspaper, writing in part, "No Christian man should be indifferent to the welfare of three millions of men held in bondage, and who were denied the reading of the Bible, and whose wives and children were liable to be sold and separated to gratify the avarice of their pretended owners."[11]

Thompson crisscrossed the state in support of freedom for Black Americans, frequently speaking at multiple venues on a given Sunday, sometimes even walking from one meeting to another. He was among those who, while speaking in New Bedford, influenced the escaped slave Frederick Douglass to take on a public role in the antislavery cause. In April 1844, while the leader of South Dedham's Universalists, Thompson spoke alongside Douglass at a meeting of the Norfolk County Anti-Slavery Society held in Dedham. Throughout the decades prior to and during the Civil War, Thompson's home in East Walpole was a welcome stop for escaping enslaved people.

On April 8, 1842, Edwin Thompson married Roxa Ellis Morse. Roxa Ellis, the daughter of Royal and Betsey Ellis of South Dedham, was born in 1813. Previously married to Joseph Morse of Walpole, who had died in

1839, Roxa had one child, Cynthia J. Morse. Roxa Ellis Morse Thompson died in 1848, only six years after their marriage. Edwin and Roxa Thompson had no children, but ten-year-old Cynthia Morse continued to live with her stepfather. In 1849, Reverend Thompson married Louisa Jane Fisher of Franklin. They had one child, Charles M. Thompson, born in 1856. Louisa Fisher Thompson passed away in 1871, and the following March, Susan M. Fisher (the sister of Louisa Fisher) became Thompson's third wife. Reverend Edwin Thompson died in his East Walpole home on May 22, 1888, at the age of seventy-nine. His widow, Susan Fisher Thompson, died on August 4, 1899. Reverend Thompson, his three wives, son and stepdaughter are interred in Norwood. Considered a giant among reformists of the early nineteenth century—he was a champion of the total abstinence movement and donated generously to support the Irish people during the Great Famine—Reverend Edwin Thompson no doubt inspired many South Dedham recruits to join the noble cause.

In his history of the town, Francis Tinker identified forty-six men who enlisted in defense of the Union for three years and thirty-nine others who signed up for nine months. Of all these men, some twenty were discharged due to sickness or wounds before the war ended; three were taken prisoner. All were, again according to Tinker, "humble men and filled no high stations" but sons of the village and probably known by most who lived in Tiot.

Just as the war began, however, there was a death in South Dedham that might also be attributed to the conflict. It occurred on a June day in 1861. Company F of the Eighteenth Massachusetts Volunteer Regiment, which was called the "First Dedham Company," as most of its recruits were from the area, arrived in South Dedham for a review and parade before heading off to battle. At the time, there was a large cannon in the village, which the men of Tiot brought to a high sand bank at the juncture of Railroad Avenue and Hill Street (later the site of the Fales Grain Mill, near today's senior housing complex). They began to fire it off in salute as the train carrying the soldiers pulled into the depot. Then tragedy struck.

Among those firing the cannon was Elijah Jones, a thirty-six-year-old cabinetmaker (furniture maker or woodworker) who lived in South Dedham with his wife, Louisa, and three daughters, Maria, Marietta and baby Hannah. As the story was told, Jones was supposed to ram powder into the cannon in preparation for its firing. None of the men participating had military experience, and they were unaware that the weapon might overheat if fired repeatedly in rapid succession. Using a wooden ramrod borrowed from a nearby foundry, Jones plunged the powder into the cannon, and it

Left: Reverend Edwin Thompson was a Universalist minister, well-known temperance leader and dedicated abolitionist. *OPPV Collection*.

Right: The stone of Elijah Jones is a striking example of the funerary urn and willow motif popular in the nineteenth century. *OPPV Collection*.

exploded unexpectedly, blowing off his hand and part of his arm. Despite the best efforts of the assembled crowd and two doctors who came as rapidly as possible, Elijah Jones died as a result of his injuries. The ramrod was later found nearly one-quarter mile away on Vernon Street. The authorities recorded his cause of death as "gunshot wound, accidental discharge of cannon." Thus, in a way, Elijah Jones was South Dedham's first casualty of the Civil War. He was buried in the cemetery on the top of the hill, his stone facing east, toward the site of his death.[12]

There are sixteen Civil War veterans interred in the cemetery, four of whom were killed during the conflict. The first combat loss to strike the village was the death of Willard F. Rhoads. Born May 10, 1838, Willard was the son of Lewis S. Rhoads and his wife, Harriet Fisher Rhoads. Lewis S. Rhoads, born in nearby Sharon, was both a farmer and a furniture maker. He was also a deacon of the South Church. Willard Rhoads joined

Company B of the First Michigan Cavalry Regiment on August 23, 1861, for three years' service. Part of the famed Michigan Brigade—referred to as the "Wolverines"—which was led for a time by George Armstrong Custer, the unit was organized in Detroit, Michigan, between August and September 1861.

The Wolverines were instrumental in many battles throughout the war, including the Battle of Gettysburg in July 1863. In June 1863, just prior to that fierce encounter, Rhoads was promoted to the rank of quartermaster sergeant. He was killed in action in Centerville, Virginia, on November 6, 1863. Both Francis Tinker's history and extant cemetery records contend that Rhoads was shot from his horse by "guerrillas." Willard Rhoads's name is etched on the family gravestone; nearby stands his official Civil War regimental marker. The village consoled Lewis S. Rhoads in his hour of grief, a task he, as deacon, had performed for many others. A deacon for over thirty-five years and a church member for more than fifty years, the elder Rhoads passed away in 1889, having outlived his son by more than a quarter of a century.

Less than a year after Willard Rhoads's death, another well-regarded South Dedham family suffered the devastating loss of two young men: the son and son-in-law of Reverend Harrison Greenough Park. Park, the son of a minister himself, was born in Providence, Rhode Island, in 1806. Following his graduation from Brown University in 1824, he studied both theology and law; he was also involved in various business establishments throughout his lifetime. Park was ordained as a minister of the South Church of Dedham in 1829, just after the Universalist schism that had brought the church's membership down from ninety-nine to thirty-eight.

In 1830, he married Julia Bird, the daughter of George Bird, who was a paper manufacturer in East Walpole. Harrison and Julia had four children: Abigail, George, Harrison Jr. and Wisner, all born in South Dedham. Sadly, Julia Bird Park died in 1835, and a few months later, Park left the South Church. For a time, he formed a partnership in a paper mill with his father-in-law and brothers-in-law, Josiah and Francis Bird, but retired from the business in 1840. He went on to serve brief pastorates in Danvers, Burlington and Bernardston, Massachusetts, and Westminster, Vermont. While in Bernardston, he was regarded as "a talented and able preacher" but one whose pastoral success was limited by his business interests. Park became a traveling agent for *Mother's Magazine*, took on the editorship of the publication *Mother's and Father's Manual* and published his own book, *A Voice from the Parsonage*, in 1854.[13]

He eventually returned to Norwood and occasionally preached at local services. Harrison G. Park died in 1876.

Harrison Park had married a second time in 1837 to Elizabeth Bird, another daughter of George Bird and the sister of his first wife. Elizabeth gave birth to several children. Julia, Henry, Montgomery, Hannah, Arabella Elizabeth and Francis were buried with their parents in this lot. The eldest child of this second marriage, Julia B. Park, was named after Elizabeth's sister and Park's first wife. In 1863, when she was twenty-five, Julia Park married John Henry Hale, a young carpenter from Bernardston, Massachusetts, a community where her father had served as pastor. On August 21 that year, John Hale enlisted and was mustered into Company I of the Ninth Massachusetts Regiment, an experienced unit. In April 1864, now led by Colonel Patrick Guiney, an Irish immigrant and Boston lawyer, the regiment received orders to join the command of Lieutenant General Ulysses S. Grant. On May 5, 1864, Company I engaged in the Battle of the Wilderness, which was a particularly ferocious confrontation. The Ninth Massachusetts suffered severely, including the loss of Private John Hale, who had been married for less than a year. Etched into one side of the Park family obelisk is the inscription: "JOHN HENRY HALE / member of Co. I 9th Regt. MVM / Slain in battle of the Wilderness / May 8, 1864 AE 27 yrs." There is a marker for John H. Hale at the Fredericksburg National Cemetery in Virginia, as well as a memorial to John and his brother James (who died during the war in New Bern, North Carolina, in 1862), in the Center Cemetery in Bernardston, Massachusetts. Julia Park Hale never remarried; she died in 1921 at the age of eighty-three, certainly one of the oldest Civil War widows in Norwood.

The Harrison G. Park family suffered another great loss only a month later. Elizabeth and Harrison's son Henry Martin Park, twenty, enlisted in the Fortieth Massachusetts Volunteers, a regiment organized at Camp Stanton in Lynnfield, Massachusetts, in August 1862. He mustered in for a three-year enlistment. Stationed primarily near Washington, D.C., the unit marched in pursuit of Lee to Berlin, Maryland, in July 1863; sailed to Folly Island, South Carolina, in August that year; and was in Hilton Head, South Carolina, during January 1864. By May 1864, the regiment was back in the Richmond, Virginia area, where it engaged in a series of battles near Bermuda Hundred, Virginia.

On May 20, 1864, Henry Park was struck by an enemy's bullet. According to a later account, despite this wound, he stood his ground and continued to fire. Hit a second time below the knee, he was forced to leave the battlefield,

Congregational minister Harrison G. Park lost both a son, Henry Park, and son-in-law, John Hale, to the American Civil War. *OPPV Collection.*

but before reaching shelter, he was hit a third time. Gravely wounded, Park was taken to the hospital at Fort Monroe, Virginia, where he died on June 18, 1864. His body was returned to South Dedham and interred in the Park family's lot almost a year later.

Near the center of the cemetery, at the edge of a slight rise in the grassy slope, three brothers are memorialized by marble regimental markers. Charles, Benjamin, and Eugene Phipps grew up in South Dedham. Their father, Loami Phipps, was a cabinet maker likely employed at the Everett Furniture Factory. Charles and Benjamin, 25 and 19, respectively, enlisted into the Twenty-fourth Massachusetts Regiment within a week of each other in September, 1861. Benjamin, who listed his occupation as a varnisher and probably worked at the Everett factory with his father, mustered into Company C on September 12. A week later, Charles, a teamster, joined Company A of the same regiment.

Although the Twenty-Fourth Massachusetts was splintered and assigned to different brigades for much of the war, on May 1, 1864, the companies were reunited in Virginia. From August 14 to August 16, 1864, the regiment fought in the battle of Deep Bottom, Virginia. Among the soldiers killed in action on August 16 was Charles W. Phipps, the eldest of the Phipps brothers. Less than a month later, Benjamin was mustered out. Lastly, Eugene (his given name was Amos Eugene) Phipps, only fifteen, was signed into the Rhode Island Light Artillery (RILA) unit on March 16, 1865. When the war ended, his company was disbanded, and Eugene was discharged on June 14, 1865.

In July 1866, only a little more than a year after the war ended, twenty-four-year-old Benjamin Phipps died of sunstroke. Eugene Phipps became a house painter and lived most of his life in Boston. In 1907, he died at the age of fifty-six as the result of an accidental fall. The veterans' father, Loami, who died in 1870, and their mother, Loriana, who passed away in 1876, are interred in unmarked graves in the family lot. Laura Phipps, the youngest of the Phipps siblings, who died in 1863 of scarlet fever at the age of six, has a small gravestone beside those of her brothers. The names of the three brothers were mistakenly omitted from the Civil War Veterans Roll of Honor in Norwood's town hall when the tablets were installed in 1928. On November 11, 2020, their names were added, and their service was recognized.

While the War Between the States raged, daily life in South Dedham went on, and the families who were left behind coped as best they could. Although they were safe from combat, deaths continued to mount in the village. In fact, the cemetery saw the highest number of burials in its history between 1861 and 1864. Several of these deaths left a lasting impact on the community.

Oramal F. Cheney, who was born in Vermont in 1826, was a cabinetmaker and superintendent for South Dedham furniture makers Haley, Morse and

Boyden, which, by the 1860s, was located next to the Smith tannery near the tracks on Railroad Avenue. The firm made mahogany extension tables and, according to several sources, was known as the first maker of rubber roller clothes-wringers in the country. In 1860, Cheney, then thirty-three, lived in South Dedham with his wife, Mary, thirty-four, and their two daughters, Adeline, eleven, and Effie, two. In April 1861, Mary gave birth to a son, Henry. She contracted puerperal fever following childbirth and died. A week later, at only fourteen days old, baby Henry, who had failed to thrive, passed away as well.

In December 1862, tragedy struck the family yet again. Still employed at Haley, Morse and Boyden, Oramal Cheney, needing some benzine, took a lantern in the gathering darkness and headed to an outdoor tank to obtain some of the liquid. Somehow, the benzine tank exploded. Cheney was severely burned and died from his injuries. Less than two years later, in February 1864, his daughter Adeline, who had been cared for by Lewis and Anna Day, died from a bowel obstruction at the age of fourteen. Oramal and Mary and their children Henry and Adeline are all interred in the cemetery. The Cheneys' remaining child, Effie, who was only four when her father's death left her an orphan, was taken in by relatives in Vermont.

Haley, Morse and Boyden was not the only furniture maker in South Dedham. Willard Everett and Company had its beginnings as a small shop; it was reorganized in 1854 and built a large three-story factory specializing in mahogany and black walnut furniture. The success of Everett's brought the first influx of immigrants to South Dedham, as talented artisans and wood carvers from southern Germany sought employment there. The business became one of the most important in South Dedham, with more than three hundred workers at its peak. When a spectacular fire destroyed the plant in 1865, Everett's relocated to Boston. Cheney's employer, Haley, Morse and Boyden, ceased operations shortly thereafter as well when their skilled craftsmen followed the larger firm to the city.

Left behind, however, are four graves bearing witness to the lives of these early immigrants. Peter Wagner, Johauss Hurst, Charles Hensel

The Oramal Cheney family was struck by a series of tragedies in the 1860s. *OPPV Collection.*

Found across the cemetery from its original location, the obelisk of Peter Wagner was returned to its base by volunteers. *OPPV Collection.*

and William Killian were each born in Germany. Wagner and Killian were cabinetmakers and Hensel was a varnisher, and they were all likely employed at Everett's factory. Hurst was a barkeep, an occupation and business common within any immigrant population. They all died within two years of each other. First, while swimming in one of Tiot's many waterways on a hot summer day, Peter Wagner, thirty-nine, and Johauss Hurst, twenty-five, accidentally drowned on August 17, 1862. The two others, Charles Hensel, who had become a naturalized citizen in 1860, and William Killian, both under the age of forty, died from tuberculosis in 1862 and 1864, respectively. Tuberculosis, then often called consumption, was the scourge of both the native-born and immigrant population in the nineteenth century. The four men were interred, with marble stones marking their graves. At some later date, all were damaged by vandals, but volunteers are working to restore the stones.

At the crest of the hill, near the graves of these men of whom little is known, stands a third small tombstone that pays tribute to the sons of yet another German immigrant. This stone, cleaned to a bright white by volunteers, reads:

OUR ALLIE.
ALFRED T. BOCK
died July 11, 1863.
aged 1 year 11 mos
25 days

—

THOMAS E. BOCK
died
June 12, 1863
aged 4 mos.

It must have been a heartbreaking year for the family. The cause of Allie's death was listed as cholera infantum; the cause of Thomas's demise is unknown. Both boys were born to Theodore Bock, a carver who was born in Germany, and Miriam Armstrong Bock, who was born in England. That is all that is known about the family.

In addition to tuberculosis, a disease that stalked some in Tiot in the 1860s was typhoid fever, an acute illness caused by a bacterium that is transmitted to humans by drinking or eating contaminated food or water. Once the bacteria reach the bloodstream, different organs may be affected, including the liver, spleen, gallbladder, lungs, kidneys and gastrointestinal tract. Symptoms of typhoid may include high fever, headache and diarrhea, which can, in turn, spread contamination further, especially among those in close or overcrowded quarters. Even if a victim recovers, there may be lingering effects or damage to the organs.

In the first few years of the 1860s, more than half a dozen South Dedham residents died of typhoid fever. They ranged in age from nine to fifty-seven, were men and women, native-born and immigrant. Jacob Felt, who was thirty-five at the time of his death, was a cabinetmaker born in Germany. Cyrus Fairbanks, thirty-seven, was a third-generation Tiot resident and grandson of Captain Abel Everett. Sybil Guild Ide was the granddaughter of Abner Guild. Guild had founded the village's first tannery; the mammoth Winslow tannery stood on the same site for more than a century, just off the Wrentham Road (today's Walpole Street).

One family hit hard by typhoid was that of Benjamin Morse. Born in South Dedham on November 7, 1806, Benjamin's parents were Seth Morse and Irene Rhoads Morse. His grandparents were Eliphalet Rhoads and Mercy Holland Rhoads. Morse became a currier, working in the leather trade. In 1829, he married Sybil Lewis, the daughter of Joseph and Sybil Lewis. Benjamin and Sybil had six children. Benjamin's wife, Sybil Morse, died of typhoid fever on January 1, 1862, at the age of fifty-two, and in December that year, his daughter Ella, nine, died of the same disease. Two years later, in 1864, Benjamin Morse died of a liver complaint, which may have been the result of his exposure to typhoid. He was fifty-seven. The disease continued to haunt the village. In 1900, there was a severe outbreak, during which forty-four people contracted typhoid; fortunately, none of them died. The source of the infection was traced to a local dairy farm, where milk had been stored in a well that was found to be polluted; the remaining milk was disposed of, and the well was filled in.

Surviving both combat and rampant disease (more Civil War troops died of disease than battle wounds) the majority of South Dedham's soldiers returned to their homes after peace was declared. Five of those interred in the cemetery were not village born; J.B. Fuller, James E. Hawes, Andrew J. Keene, Leonard Lowell and Lewis G. Stone became associated with the town later in life. Fuller, born in Walpole, was a currier who worked at the tannery; he died in 1895. James Hawes was born in Wrentham. Andrew Keene grew up in Pembroke, Massachusetts, was a bootmaker by trade and lived most of his life in Sharon and Stoughton. Leonard Lowell was a Maine native. A few years after the war, he married Frances Gay, a South Dedham native and daughter of local veterinarian Jarvis Gay; he was buried not far from his wife's family. Finally, Lewis Stone was a machinist who arrived when the New York and New England Railroad car shops relocated to the town in 1876. In later years, he lived in Roslindale and was employed at the Registry of Deeds. He died tragically in 1907, when he was struck by a fire engine.

The rest of Old Parish's Civil War veterans were born and raised in South Dedham. Young men with little or no knowledge of the world outside their village, they were akin to the naïve boys referenced in Thornton Wilder's *Our Town*: they "had a notion that the Union ought to be kept together, though they'd never seen more than fifty miles of it themselves."[14] Among those who enlisted for three years, Sumner Ellis, a laborer and farmer,

This Civil War regimental marker memorializes Willard F. Rhodes. The nearby family gravestone spells his name Willard F. Rhoads. *OPPV Collection.*

was wounded during the Second Battle of Bull Run on August 30, 1862; following his recovery, he reenlisted and served to the end of the war. Alfred Ellis and Albert Ellis (not siblings) both joined Company I of the Thirty-Fifth Massachusetts Regiment. They fought at Antietam, one of the fiercest battles of the war, where Alfred was wounded but remained with his unit. Following a winter encampment in Virginia and then action in Mississippi, Kentucky and Tennessee, the regiment returned to Virginia. Both were mustered out in June 1865.

Nine months men William H. Gay and Charles J. Guild, both cabinetmakers, had enlisted together in August 1862, trained at Readville, Massachusetts, and were stationed near New Bern, North Carolina, for much of their tour. They were mustered out on July 30, 1863, after a two-month delay. William Gay went on to became an active member of the George K. Bird Post No. 169 of the Grand Army of the Republic, founded in 1884 and headquartered in Norwood. Elected an officer of the post in 1900, Gay led members of the organization as they gathered at Old Parish Cemetery each Memorial Day to place wreaths at the graves of their comrades. He was one of the longest-lived of Norwood's Civil War veterans; his gravestone bears the insignia of the Grand Army of the Republic. This emblem and the regimental markers at the graves of Willard Rhoads, J.B. Fuller and the Phipps brothers are the only reminder of the sacrifice these young men made for the village of South Dedham and the United States.

6

FAMILIES AND COMMUNITY

A bove all else, the approximately two-acre graveyard that is Old Parish Cemetery is the final resting place of individuals and families who, together, created a community. They were farmers, tanners, blacksmiths and grocers. They ran mills, taverns and schools. They were ministers, teachers, doctors and soldiers. Some had eccentricities that were accepted with affection; others faced tragedy that was assuaged by friends and neighbors. There are no famous women or men buried here, only ordinary people who made their own way in the world. They supported their village and country, loved their children and prayed to their God. They deserve to be remembered. These are a few of their stories.

Alvin L. Ellis was born in South Dedham in 1819. He was the son of Isaac Ellis and Abigail Fairbanks Ellis. He married Martha B. Dean in 1840. Alvin and Martha had twelve children. The family was plagued by tuberculosis, then referred to as consumption. It was a very common disease and, even at the turn of the twentieth century, was the leading cause of death in the United States. Alvin, Martha and several of their adult children died of the disease. One son, Alfred B. Ellis, was a minister; one daughter, Abby F., was a schoolteacher. During most of his adult life, Alvin L. Ellis worked as a butcher, packer, teamster and, in 1870, depot master for the railroad. When the new town of Norwood was founded in 1872, Alvin Ellis became its first official town pound keeper.

Just about every town in New England had a pound. In fact, a pound was so necessary to the orderly functioning of a community that they were required by law. If an animal strayed and was found destroying private property, it was brought to the pound, where it was corralled with other wayward creatures and watched over by a town-appointed pound keeper (sometimes called a pound master or pounder) until its owner could retrieve it for a fee. Beginning in the 1840s, South Dedham's pound was located on Nahatan Street, near the corner of today's School Street. It remained at the same site when Norwood was incorporated.

Alvin Ellis was the pound keeper for Norwood until his death on January 8, 1876, his wife having predeceased him on August 15, 1869. All that remains of the town pound today is an uneven patch of land and a stone ledge pierced by a few iron staples, which was once used to hold the animal pens in place.

***

Ebenezer Fisher Talbot was born in 1814 and died on June 9, 1882, of heart disease at the age of sixty-eight. His wife, Elizabeth Farrington Talbot, was born in 1817 and died on February 15, 1895, of pneumonia. The couple lost four young children between 1845 and 1860: Mary Elizabeth died in 1845 at the age of eight; Josiah Fisher died in 1847 at the age of ten weeks; Sarah Amanda died in 1855 at the age of one; and Eugene died in infancy in 1860. Their sole surviving son, Samuel R. Talbot, died in 1878 at the age of twenty-four of diabetes, a disease for which there was no cure or even treatment at that time.

Talbot was a successful businessman with an excellent reputation in South Dedham. He began to manufacture oilcloth around 1850, and a few years later, he established a manufacturing facility off Railroad Avenue, where he produced printed flooring and carriage oilcloths. The Hill Street area, overlooking the railroad tracks and depot at the juncture of Railroad Avenue and Hill Street, rapidly became known as Carpet Shop Hill.

In the late 1860s, a disgruntled employee burned the business down along with Talbot's home; both were rebuilt, only to have a second accidental fire destroy both yet again. Talbot's South Dedham neighbors helped him build a third factory on the original site and a home on the Washington Street property owned by his brother.

Ebenezer Fisher Talbot continued to produce carpet cloth until his death, after which the business was taken over by E.E. Pratt and Son, an enterprise

With the supervision of OPPV volunteers, Boy Scouts uncovered, repaired and reset individual small markers in the Ebenezer Fisher Talbot family lot. *OPPV Collection*.

that employed twenty men and produced 180,000 yards of carpeting annually. Pratt and Son was eventually purchased by Chandler and Gay Company, which ran the business until 1900.

***

Benjamin D. Guild was born on October 25, 1827. His parents were Nathanial Guild, a farmer, and Sybil Hewins Guild. Nathanial's father (Benjamin's grandfather) was Abner Guild, the tannery founder. Nathanial and Sybil Guild had seven children. The couple's third child and third son, Benjamin, never married. He spent time at the Taunton Hospital, an asylum for the unstable, in the 1870s, but in 1879, he apparently found his calling when the Town of Norwood built its first municipal building: a "lock-up for tramps."

The arrival of the railroad was advantageous to industries in South Dedham, but it also brought problems, including transients who rode the railroad cars from town to town and often depended on charity or petty larceny to sustain themselves. As part of their "support to the poor," towns were required to provide food and lodging for these homeless travelers. In 1876, only a few years after Norwood had become an independent town, the annual report stated: "The excess on the Poor is due largely to the increased number of Tramps, which now have to be put up at the hotel. The selectmen would recommend that the town take some action in regard to the matter, so that it will not cost as much in the future." In 1876, the town cared for 1,372 transients; in 1877, that number rose to 2,843. In 1879, the town appropriated $1,250 to build a lock-up to house the poor.

From 1879 until his death a decade later, Benjamin Guild became the "tramp keeper." Each annual report mentions an amount for the board and clothing of travelers overseen by Benjamin, who was, at times, referred to as "General Guild" or "Major-General Guild." In 1889, the annual report noted, "Ben Guild has cared for 2,936 tramps during the year."

When Benjamin D. Guild died on September 10, 1889, of a hemorrhage caused by tuberculosis, the *Norwood Advertiser and Review* wrote, "The town has lost a unique citizen and faithful official and a member of one of the old-time honored families. 'Major General' Guild, as he was called by those who were familiar with his military precision and dispatch, although he never engaged more than a civilian's honor, performed well all his duties in that direction. Ever since the establishment of the town 'lock-up' in 1879, he has had entire charge, conducting its affairs in a manner highly satisfactory to the town fathers." Benjamin Guild, sixty-two, was survived by two brothers. He was buried in the family plot.[15]

In 1903, steel cells were added to the lock-up to hold prisoners awaiting transportation to the Dedham Courthouse. The building housed prisoners for some eighty-five years. Late in the twentieth century, the building was the site of the youth coordinator's office. Today, the lockup still stands behind the town hall but is now used primarily for storage.

***

Eliphalet Fales III was born on May 24, 1780. On June 20, 1804, Eliphalet Fales III married Sibyl Sumner, the daughter of George Sumner and Margaret Lewis Sumner, also of Dedham. Eliphalet and Sibyl had nine children, including three daughters named Harriet. The first child named Harriet died just before turning three years old; the next was less than a year old when she died; the third, Harriet Newell Fales, lived to adulthood and married Benjamin Fuller of Sharon. Their other children were Horace, Charlotte, Eliphalet Newman, Mentor, Olive and John Sumner Fales.

Olive Fales, who died in 1876, purchased this gravestone to memorialize her parents, her siblings and herself. *OPPV Collection*.

Eliphalet Fales III was a farmer in South Dedham. He died on September 5, 1848, of dysentery. His wife, Sibyl Sumner Fales, died on November 4, 1867, in Walpole of old age. They are interred in the cemetery along with their children. There are two memorials situated in the lot, both large marble stones. On one is recorded the birth and death dates of Eliphalet III; his wife, Sibyl; and three of their daughters, Charlotte Fales Smith, who married Seth Ellison Smith in 1828 and had four daughters of her own; Harriet Fales, who died in 1815, a few months before her third birthday; and Olive Fales. Olive never married and died in 1876 of paralysis. As inscribed on the marble stone, it was Olive "who gave this stone," thus commemorating the family.

Nearby stands the reset stone of two of Eliphalet and Sibyl's sons: Mentor Fales and John Sumner Fales. Both were farmers; neither ever married. Mentor passed away on July 12, 1893; his death was attributed to old age. John S. Fales died on September 18, 1897, of a brain disease. He had been in poor health for several years. Another son, Horace Fales, and his family are interred in a separate lot in the cemetery.

Finally, their son Eliphalet Newman, known as Newman, married Lucy Bullard Weatherbee in 1845. They had eight children, including Frank Aldrich Fales. In 1877, Frank Fales purchased the grain and feed business of William Fisher. In 1880, he built a large complex on Railroad Avenue, from which he ran an extensive business in flour, grain, meal, feed, hay and similar commodities. He was elected to the Norwood Board of Selectmen in 1882 and held that position for twenty years. He also represented the district in the Massachusetts House of Representatives from 1886 to 1888 and again from 1900 to 1902. At some point, the bodies of Newman, his wife and children, which were interred in this cemetery, were moved to Highland Cemetery, where the bodies of Frank A. Fales and his wife, Jennie Train Fales, were also buried.

The two large gravestones belonging to the Eliphalet Fales III family now stand at the top of the hill, overlooking what was once the site of his grandson Frank A. Fales's thriving business.

***

Sumner Ellis was born in South Dedham in 1843; his parents were Paul Ellis and Jane Sumner Ellis. In the 1860 U.S. census, at the age of eighteen, he was recorded as living with his parents and several siblings. Also living in the household was Catherine Cuff, sixteen, who was born in Ireland. She was among the first Irish immigrants who came to South Dedham and found work, as many young, single Irish women did, as a domestic servant.

Badly damaged by vandals, the stone of Sumner, Catherine and Henry Ellis was repaired, reset and cleaned by volunteers. *OPPV Collection.*

On July 3, 1861, Sumner Ellis, then nineteen years old and working as a moulder, enlisted as a private in Company F of the Eighteenth Massachusetts Regiment. Ellis was wounded at the Second Battle of Bull Run, Virginia, in 1862. Discharged for his injuries, Ellis recuperated and re-enlisted on January 12, 1864. He was discharged with disability on June 17, 1865. Upon his return to South Dedham, Sumner Ellis married Catherine Cuff. In 1870, Sumner and Catherine were still living in the Paul Ellis household; the young husband was working at the tannery, and his wife was "sewing straw."

A cottage industry that flourished in the mid-nineteenth century, the local straw factory stood on Cottage Street, just off the village center. Hay would be transported to this building, where it was braided into long strands. Subsequently, women throughout the village would pick up both these braided strings and hat molds, return to their homes and construct straw hats. Local historian Win Everett described the process in a 1933 *Norwood Messenger* article:

> *The braided straw was put in a bucket of water to soak. Then the mold was held in the lap and the hat started in the center of the crown on the top of the mold. The straw was, of course, sewed around in concentric circles, working it over the edge of the crown and tightly down the sides of the mold to get the shape. When the head of the bonnet was thus sewed, a separate piece was sewed on for the flaring edge and the outside edge neatly finished. Then the mold was set away to dry. When the dry straw was removed from the mold, the shape of the hat was fixed.*

There is no definitive list of home laborers so employed, but a perusal of the 1870 U.S. census indicates almost two dozen village women (and girls), like Catherine Cuff Ellis, listed their occupation as "sewing straw."

Sumner and Catherine Ellis had two sons: Frank and Henry. Frank Ellis was born in 1867, and in 1872, a second son, Henry W. Ellis, was born. Tragically, Henry died of tuberculosis on October 12, 1873, at only nine months of age. A year later, Catherine Cuff Ellis died at the age of thirty of the same disease. Sumner Ellis never remarried. He died suddenly of heart disease on January 11, 1897, at the age of fifty-four. According to the *Norwood Advertiser and Review*, Ellis was a "man of pleasant disposition and kindly heart." The funeral was held at the home of his surviving son, Frank S. Ellis. His remains were interred in the Old Parish Cemetery alongside those of his wife, Catherine, and his son Henry (see the image on page 84).

***

According to historian and newspaperman Win Everett, Lem Dean was "one of the most picturesque characters who ever brightened the life of our village." Born in 1795 in the John Dean homestead, Lemuel Dean was part of the expansive Dean family. He married Julia Ann Morse around 1830. The couple had seven children: Charles E., Rene, Lyman, Lewis, Henry, an unnamed infant and a second child named Charles.

In 1824, Dean was the tax collector in Tiot, but in 1828, when the South Church was preparing to build its third meetinghouse, he bought the tavern on Washington Street that had belonged to Abel Everett, moved it across to the corner of today's Chapel Street and opened a general store of sorts. His stock was apparently meagre, but he usually had molasses, vinegar, rum, gin, a few spices and a little sugar. Always dressed in a black suit and tall black beaver hat, Dean was known to move about the store at a snail's pace. Francis O. Winslow recalled, "Lem could take longer than any living man to go into the cellar and draw a jug of molasses." Even more memorable, Dean always carried a supply of skunk skins in the store, which came from skunks that he hunted, skinned and tacked to the building's clapboards to dry in the sun. Consequently, the store—and Lem Dean—perpetually had the odor of skunk about them.

In later years, Dean sold the store and built a house on Lenox Avenue. Still, he would fill a pushcart or sometimes a wheelbarrow with peanuts and skunk skins and walk the streets of South Dedham, selling his odd merchandise. Writing in the 1930s, Win Everett says he found a few old-timers who remembered the foul-smelling "little bit of a man" with a round face and high-pitched voice, peddling his wares. He was, they conceded, "a gentle, harmless soul."

Lemuel Dean died in 1880; his wife, Julia, lived a decade longer and passed away in 1890. They were buried in Old Parish Cemetery along with five of their children, all of whom died under the age of seven.

Born in the Dean homestead on June 14, 1797, Mary Dean was the younger sister of Lemuel Dean. Mary taught school in Sharon, Walpole, West Dedham and South Dedham, where she taught at both the Old Brick Schoolhouse on Pleasant Street and the Clapboardtree District School at the northern end of the village. She resigned from teaching when, at the age of twenty-eight, she married Dean Chickering on December 14, 1825. It was a notable coincidence that the Christian name of her husband was identical to her maiden surname: Dean Chickering married Mary Dean.

This stone is inscribed to merchant Lemuel Dean; his wife, Julia; and their five young children. *OPPV Collection.*

Chickering was a widower with one daughter at the time of their marriage. Dean Chickering and Mary Dean Chickering lived in the house at the head of Hoyle Street on the Wrentham Road; the house became known as the Chickering Place and is still standing on the corner of Chickering Road and

Walpole Street. The couple had one son, John Dean Chickering. Eventually, Mary Dean Chickering came to know three grandchildren and three great-grandchildren. Dean Chickering, a dedicated member and deacon of the South Church, died at the age of sixty-five.

Throughout her life, Mary Dean Chickering was very active and never had a serious illness. In 1897, on the occasion of her one hundredth birthday, a reception was held at the Chickering home between three and five o'clock in the afternoon. More than one hundred friends and neighbors came to help her celebrate. Due to her advanced age and fragile condition, they were admitted only in small groups. The oldest woman in Norwood at that time, Mary Dean Chickering shook hands with everyone, and although her memory was not perfect, she recognized many. She was presented with a bouquet of flowers, a cake and one hundred peppermints (her favorite candy). A lengthy newspaper article noted that her habit was to get up a little before noon and spend time in her sitting room and outside in her yard in good weather. It was said that she could recall stories told to her by elderly people who remembered events that occurred long before the American Revolution. Chickering herself remembered the stagecoaching days and was amazed by the bicycles that passed her house daily; she called them "a wonder and a mystery."

Mary Dean Chickering was a kindly, good-hearted woman. Although her eyesight was impaired, even at one hundred, her hearing remained good. Less than a month after her one hundredth birthday, she passed away. It had been noted at her centenary celebration that "her life has been a quiet and useful one, and though devoid of great events, has been full of help and care for others."[16]

Mary's son, John Dean Chickering, was born in 1836. A cabinetmaker by trade, in 1856, he married Amelia H. Cokley. They had three children: Walter D., Sarah Louisa and Mary Ida. Amelia Chickering died in 1862. On January 17, 1869, John Chickering married Mary M. Currier, who was born in York, Maine. They had no children. Only four years after their marriage, Mary Currier Chickering died of tuberculosis. After that, Chickering and his children lived with his mother, Mary Dean Chickering, and John found work in the tannery. Eventually, Sarah Louisa was married; Walter and Mary Ida remained single.

In 1910, John Gillooly, who lived close to Chickering on Walpole Street, drove the seventy-four-year-old John Dean Chickering and another friend, Isaiah Merrifield, eighty-seven, to see the Harvard-Boston Great Aero Meet at Squantum, just outside the city. At the event, the men viewed a host of modern planes, including the Bleriot monoplane, operated by Graham White, and biplanes built by, among others, Wilbur Wright. As his mother had been amazed by bicycles, John Dean Chickering was overwhelmed by the sight of man-made aircraft in the sky. "It was wonderful, wonderful," he said. "I had never expected to see it."[17] John Dean Chickering died on April 18, 1915, of pneumonia. Walter Dean Chickering died in 1923 of influenza; Mary Ida Chickering died in 1950. All were buried in the Chickering family lot.

***

Ezra Morse, who was born in 1671, was one of the first settlers of the village of South Dedham when his father, also named Ezra Morse, set up a sawmill on the Neponset River sometime before 1680. Morse and his wife, the former Mary Lovett, had three sons: Ezra, John and Joseph. His daughter, Mary, married and moved away. The sons remained—as did their sons and their sons. Even the great-great-great-grandsons of Ezra Morse lived and worked in Tiot and, later, in the town of Norwood. Three of these grandsons took differing routes in their lives.

David Morse Jr. was born on August 25, 1787. He was the son of David Morse and Sibbel Ellis Morse and was descended from Ezra Morse's eldest son, Ezra. On October 22, 1814, David Morse Jr. married Nancy Gay. They had three children: Anson, Sarah and David. After the Norfolk and Bristol Turnpike (today's Washington Street) was built in 1806, David Morse Jr. opened the Morse Tavern on the turnpike in East Walpole. It has been estimated that up to twenty stagecoaches would stop at the tavern each day on their way between Boston and Providence.

In addition to being a public house and inn, the Morse Tavern became the first post office in the town of Walpole, and David Morse was appointed the first postmaster of the town. In 1847, Morse sold the tavern; two years later, his wife, Nancy Gay Morse, passed away. Following her death, Morse lived with his daughter, Sarah R. Morse, and her husband, Willard Everett, a partner in South Dedham's Everett Furniture Factory. He remained Walpole's postmaster until his death on September 5, 1852, of kidney disease.

Francis Morse was born on April 28, 1821. His parents were John Morse and Roxa Fuller Morse, and he was descended from Ezra Morse's son John. Following in the footsteps of that branch of the family, Francis Morse was a miller, with his home and mill situated at the southern edge of South Dedham, bordering Walpole, on today's abandoned Water Street.

Francis Morse married Mary Nye Snow in 1851 in Worcester. They had two children: John F., born in 1852, and Mary N., born in 1854. Mary Snow Morse died on March 17, 1854; she was only thirty years old. On February 9, 1858, Francis Morse married for a second time. Lucie Grogan had been born in 1830 in Maine. This second marriage brought three more children into the family: Belle, born in 1859; Percy, born in 1860; and Jennie, born in 1868.

Francis Morse continued to list his occupation as proprietor of a gristmill—like his great-great-great-grandfather—until the 1880 census. He died on December 20, 1885, from cancer. His widow, Lucie Grogan Morse, died on November 29, 1913, of pneumonia. Francis Morse and both his wives are interred in the Morse family plot at Old Parish Cemetery (see the image on page 52).

George H. Morse is a name familiar to many in Norwood. Born on February 12, 1834, to Joseph and Millie Dean Morse, he was descended from two longtime South Dedham families: the Deans and the Morses. George was descended from Ezra Morse's son Joseph. George H. Morse became a farmer on the flat, fertile plain in the southern part of South Dedham. He married Abigail "Abbie" Rawson Shackley in 1855 in Walpole, where Abbie had been born. The couple had two daughters: Ellen Florence and Catherine "Katie" Lilian. Abbie R. Morse, thirty-four, passed away due to cancer on February 21, 1869, a short time after the couple had built an Italianate-style home on Washington Street. Two years later, in May 1871, George H. Morse married Althine Atkins.

In addition to being a farmer, George H. Morse gained some local fame as an auctioneer. He also acquired considerable property through his dealings in real estate. Morse was a member of the Orient Lodge of Masons, belonged to the Tiot Lodge of Odd Fellows and was a member of both the South Dedham and the Norwood Brass Band. Deeply involved in local politics, he was one of the first members of Norwood's Board of Assessors in 1872, when the town was formed. He was also chief engineer of the fire department, served as a surveyor of lumber and highways and was on the Board of Selectmen from 1877 to 1893.

Morse's second wife, Althine Atkins, died on November 14, 1896, of liver cancer. George H. Morse passed away on May 6, 1917. He was eighty-three years old, and although he died of arterio sclerosis, he had been very active until a few days prior to his death. He was survived by his daughter E. Florence Morse. His only other child, his daughter Katie Morse, who was a teacher, had died in 1879 at the age of twenty-one.

By the time of George H. Morse's death in 1917, the cemetery and the community had entered a new phase. The village of South Dedham had become the town of Norwood; its population, now much more diverse, had soared from approximately two thousand in 1872 to ten thousand in 1917. And a new cemetery had been established. The former parish burial ground was gradually becoming obsolete.

7

OBSOLESCENCE

B y the 1870s, the Old Parish Cemetery had reached its peak in beauty and, perhaps, usefulness. The slate gravestones of the eighteenth century had been joined by ever taller and more substantial marble monuments. The large lots of the wealthiest families were encircled by granite coping and elaborate wrought-iron fencing. When a series of stereopticon photographs of significant Norwood sites was produced, two views of the cemetery were included. And yet, the graveyard was hemmed in by parcels of private property and a working tannery. Even as the village of South Dedham became the town of Norwood, it was already apparent that these few acres, although historic, would no longer suffice as a cemetery for the newly incorporated municipality with plans for growth.

Recognizing the imminent need, in 1878, the town purchased a little over seventeen undeveloped acres of land well west of the town center from residents Matthew Clay, John Nugent and William Cuff for future use as a cemetery. In March 1879, a cemetery committee comprising George Everett, Lewis Day, William Curtis Fisher, Ellis Draper and Francis O. Winslow, all respected and longtime citizens, was appointed and authorized to oversee the establishment of a new burial ground.

The committee chose the name Highland View Cemetery (it later became simply Highland Cemetery) and engaged Reuben T. Woodward to lay out a plan for an initial six acres of the property. Woodward was an experienced landscape gardener and horticulturalist. Born in Boston, he learned his trade from the age of seven, opening his own landscaping and gardening

A rare stereopticon view, taken by photographer Thomas Lewis, shows the cemetery at the height of its Victorian beauty. *Courtesy of the Norwood Historical Society.*

business in 1853. Following his service in the Civil War, he returned to this occupation. He was paid nearly $2,000 to design and create a modern cemetery in Norwood.

By September 1879, most of the main avenues were completed, and two hundred lots were offered for sale with a new set of regulations. Unlike the old cemetery, in this new cemetery, there would be no wall, fence, coping or hedge around the perimeter of lots, and granite posts marking their corners could extend no more than one inch aboveground. Interest was apparently immediate. Families with the means began to exchange lots in the old burying ground for spaces in what the Cemetery Committee called "this more attractive spot." By the end of 1883, some fifty-four lots had been sold. In 1887, Norwood approved the opening of a section in the cemetery for the Catholic population. (Catholics had previously been interred in diocesan cemeteries.) This decision on the part of the town opened Highland to many more residents. By the close of 1890, there had been 375 interments in the new cemetery; by comparison, during that same decade, there were 83 burials in Old Parish. Clearly, the older graveyard had become a less desirable alternative for those in need.

Some of the most affluent and influential families arranged for the disinterment and relocation of the remains of their loved ones, along with the accompanying gravestones. The bodies of the parents and grandparents of Cemetery Commissioner Lewis Day were among the first to be moved. Born in Walpole in 1807, Day's father, Joseph Day, was an entrepreneur, leather currier and state representative. He became a leader in the Universalist Society and one of the wealthiest men in South Dedham. Joseph, who died in 1876; his wife, Hannah Rhoads Day, who had predeceased him in 1863; and their infant son Joseph had been interred in the village burial ground along with Hannah's parents, Lewis and Hannah Rhoads. All were relocated to Highland Cemetery. Lyman Smith, the father of Anna Smith Day, the wife of Lewis Day, moved the remains of his first wife (Anna's mother), Melinda Guild Smith, only a few a years before his own demise in 1883.

Sometime prior to 1890, George H. Morrill, the namesake of an enormously successful ink mill, removed the remains of his first wife, Sarah; his father, Samuel; and his son Sheldon to the new cemetery. The producer of perfecting press ink, which was used by the majority of newspapers in the United States, Morrill's was considered the largest printing ink works in the world. Morrill's monument, which had been the tallest in Old Parish, was relocated as well. The graves of tannery owner George Winslow; his wife, Olive Smith Winslow; two of their children; and Olive's parents, John and Anna Smith, were all moved to Highland in 1901. Others, including some from the Fogg, Fales, Morse and Martin Winslow families followed suit, leaving empty spaces throughout the old cemetery.

Still, many of the men and women whose families had lived in the village, now a town, for generations continued to be interred in the aging graveyard. Among them was Jarvis Gay, whose death in 1882 was both shocking and tragic.[18]

As a veterinary surgeon, Jarvis Gay was often called out at all hours. In 1882, at the age of seventy-eight, he was becoming frail and was nearly deaf. According to a *Boston Globe* account of the events, at 1:15 a.m. on June 19 that year, Gay was called to attend a sick horse in the adjacent town of Canton. As he made his way home, he apparently became disoriented by the fog, which often formed along the road through the meadows on the east of town. Perhaps hoping to get directions or recognizing the house he had grown up in, Gay hitched his horse in front of what had been his father's home on Neponset Street and went up to the door. Inside, George Edmunds, a Civil War veteran and woodcarver, had only recently moved into the house with his wife and three children at the request of his elderly parents who lived there and felt they needed assistance.

Awakened by his wife and parents shouting that someone was trying to break into the house, Edmunds saw the light of a lantern flashing in the yard. He went into the kitchen and repeatedly called out, asking who was there. He got no response, just a pounding on the door and footsteps. Startled and a bit frightened, Edmunds got his father's gun, loaded it, stuck the barrel out the kitchen window and shouted, "Who's there? If you don't answer, I'll shoot!" Jarvis Gay could not hear the warning. Edmunds shot at a passing shadow. He then sat in the kitchen with the gun on his knee, still fearful that someone might again try to enter the house. At around 3:30 a.m., Edmunds's father looked out and saw a man lying on the ground. The elder Edmunds ran to a neighboring farm, and a doctor was summoned, but Jarvis Gay was dead.

An inquest was held at which another neighbor testified that he had heard Edmunds's shouted warning and the shot being fired. The Gay family, town officials and a Dedham Court judge all agreed the death was not intentional but a tragic accident. Gay simply had not heard George Edmunds calling out; instead, the confused elderly man had kept wandering with his lantern from door to door, increasing Edmunds's anxiety. The medical examiner testified that Jarvis Gay had died instantly. George Edmunds said he was "deeply sorry" for his actions. Jarvis Gay is buried in Old Parish along with his wife, Fanny L. Dean Gay, who died in 1891. George Edmunds was not interred in Old Parish Cemetery; however, his son Thomas, who passed away in 1876, was.

A short distance away is the final resting place of Jarvis and Fanny Gay's daughter Frances and her family. Frances Gay had been born in 1840 in South Dedham. On May 3, 1868, she married Leonard Lowell, who was born in Maine in 1835 and was a Civil War veteran. The young couple lived in the South Dedham area (in 1870, they were in Dedham; in 1880, they were in Walpole) and Leonard Lowell was a conductor on the railroad. In November 1868, the couple had a daughter, Alice F. Lowell; the baby died just over a year later of smallpox. In 1871, they had a son, Arthur G. Lowell, but once again, tragedy struck the Lowell family. On June 24, 1880, nine-year-old Arthur accidentally drowned.

Leonard Lowell continued to work for the railroad, and in November 1877, he was mentioned in a *Boston Globe* article when the engine of the New York and New England Railroad collided with loose cars at Franklin,

Massachusetts, resulting in the death of an engineer. An inquest was held, and it was determined that Lowell had done nothing wrong; it was another employee, who, failing to secure the cars for the night, had caused the accident. When Leonard Lowell died in 1896 of cirrhosis of the liver, the couple had been living in Woonsocket, Rhode Island, for some time, where he held a position on the street railway. Frances Gay Lowell died in 1922 and joined her husband and children in the old cemetery.

James Engles was also a relative newcomer to the village but held an official position in the years after the town's incorporation. A tinsmith and sheet iron worker by trade, Engles originally came from Provincetown, Massachusetts, but he and his wife, Susan Hutchins Engles, who were married in 1851, and their children were living in South Dedham by 1870. From 1872 to 1877, Engles was paid by the town for his repair work on furnaces, stoves, wells, oil burners, pipes and lanterns. In addition, in 1872 and 1876, Engles served the town as a constable and truant officer. A few years later, he returned to Provincetown, where he died in 1887.

On February 5, 1874, while the family was residing in Norwood, Engles's wife, Susan, died and was interred in Old Parish Cemetery, as was their daughter Marie Estelle, who died of Bright's disease in 1880. Although James Engles was married a second time, when he passed away, his body was returned to Norwood and interred with that of his first wife, Susan. When their daughter Carrie succumbed to a pulmonary disease in 1893, she, too, was buried in Old Parish with her parents and sister. In 1929, Norwood's cemetery department reported vandalism in Old Parish Cemetery. Among the stones knocked over were those belonging to the Engles family. These have since been restored and cleaned.

Another resident who played a role as the new town of Norwood assembled its first set of officials was Caleb Ellis. Born in South Dedham on February 8, 1818, Caleb Ellis's parents were Richard and Abigail E. Dean Ellis. In 1854, he married Emily A. Fuller, who was born in 1828 in Francestown, New Hampshire. In the 1860 U.S. census, Caleb Ellis's occupation was identified as "civil engineer." He was especially active in town government, holding the positions of inspector, surveyor, registrar and superintendent of streets. When Norwood was incorporated, he was one of its first three town assessors, along with Tyler Thayer and George H. Morse. In 1890, Ellis surveyed the Old Cemetery, and the town utilized his map for more than a century. Caleb and Emily Ellis had no children, and they retired to Boston. Ellis succumbed to meningitis in July 1898 at the age of eighty. More than a decade later, in 1911, Emily Ellis died

Toppled in 1929, the gravestones belonging to former constable James Engles and his family were restored in 2021. *OPPV Collection.*

tragically at their home in Boston of carbon monoxide poisoning. It was considered likely that Emily, who was suffering from senility, may have accidentally caused her own death through the mishandling of a gas light fixture. She was eighty-three. The Ellis stone is one of the largest and most impressive in the cemetery.

The impressive memorial commissioned by Caleb Ellis is decorated with an elaborate Celtic cross. *Courtesy of Halvorson | Tighe and Bond Studio.*

George Butler Talbot was born in 1820. His father, Joel Talbot, had been a veteran of the War of 1812, and his mother, Hannah Fuller Talbot, grew up in Tiot village. With his first wife, Caroline A. Robertson, Talbot had two children: Ella, born in 1855, and Albert, born in 1862. Caroline Talbot died of tuberculosis in December 1864. Only four months later, their son, Albert, died at only two years of age. In February 1866, George Talbot was married a second time to Elizabeth A. Dickey. George and Elizabeth had one child, Arthur W. Talbot, who was born in 1868.

A man active in town affairs, George B. Talbot, along with Joseph Day and Lyman Smith, formed a committee in 1863 to sell the original Universalist Society building to South Dedham's growing Roman Catholic population. The Universalists then erected a new meetinghouse at the corner of Washington and Nahatan Streets. Talbot was also among the first to sign a petition to form a new town in 1871 and deliver it to the Legislative Committee on Towns at the state house in Boston. A furniture finisher by trade, Talbot worked for both the Everett Furniture Company and Haley, Morse and Boyden for many years. Later in life, he became a farmer. Talbot was described as one of the town's best citizens and a great supporter of foreign-born newcomers to Norwood. He had been in poor health for several years prior to his death on January 26, 1898.

Subsequently, Talbot's widow, Elizabeth, and son, Arthur, moved from the family farm to a house on Guild Street in the center of town. In 1894, Ella Talbot, the daughter of George and his first wife, Caroline, was nearly forty when she married Eugene Ferrin. They were living in Chelsea when Ella passed away of tuberculosis in 1905. Her funeral was held at the home of her stepmother, and she was interred in the family plot with her parents. When Elizabeth Talbot died two years later, a lengthy obituary in the *Norwood Messenger* on May 25, 1907, noted that she "was of an amiable, kindly disposition and was a good woman in every way." Confined to her home for about eighteen months before her death, she was, again according to the *Messenger*, "a patient and cheerful sufferer during her long illness, and was cheered by the visits of friends and the faithful devotion of her son."

In 1896, two years before the deaths of Caleb Ellis and George B. Talbot, the community lost one of its most beloved residents: Francis O. Tinker. Born in Worthington, Massachusetts, Tinker lived for many years in Ashby, where he was postmaster, town clerk, librarian and writer of histories. He moved to South Dedham around 1867 and opened a small drugstore and soda fountain. In 1872, at the incorporation of Norwood, he was elected the first town clerk. Recording all official proceedings in a clear, legible hand, he held the office for twenty-three years until age and ill health forced him to resign. In addition, Tinker served as a trustee to the library and was a member of that board at its establishment as a public institution. A lover of books, especially histories, Tinker became the first historian of Norwood, publishing a sketch of the town both in a history of Norfolk County and in Norwood's resident directory of 1890. He also served as clerk for the South Church, which had become the First Congregational Church, and compiled a history of the settlement and growth of the parish.

The *Norwood Advertiser and Review*, then the only local paper, wrote on June 6, 1896:

> *He was a mild, peaceable man, but intensely patriotic, approving of war for the sake of liberty, country, honor and home, but in no other sense. In character, Tinker was quiet, sincere, conscientious, modest but firm. His words were few; his voice low and pleasant; his principles decided and humane; his religious faith unwavering, but tolerant and kindly towards that of others who differed from him. He possessed a good-natured vein of humor, enjoying a joke and a pleasant anecdote as well as anyone. Socially he was genial and pleasant, full of kindly feeling and easily moved by distress and pathos. He was an abolitionist and a Republican in politics but in no sense a politician. He had no enemies, and perhaps no man in town has so many friends.*

On November 13, 1872, shortly after Norwood's incorporation, Orra Gertrude Tinker was born (although 1873 is engraved on the memorial). She was the daughter of Charles Tinker and his wife, Ann Maria Wellington Tinker, and the granddaughter of Francis Tinker. Tragically, on March 24, 1880, seven-year-old Orra Gertrude Tinker died of meningitis. Francis Tinker's wife, Rachel Elizabeth Hutchinson Tinker, died on June 27, 1915, in Vermont. All three are interred in the Tinker family lot.

The memorial of historian Francis O. Tinker, Norwood's first town clerk, before and after cleaning. *OPPV Collection.*

James Engles, Caleb Ellis and George Talbot each had family members already interred in Old Parish when they died, and Francis Tinker, as the historian of his adopted town, had a particular affinity for the already-ages-old historic site. Perhaps that is why they chose not to be buried in the town's new cemetery. Three brothers were interred in Old Parish under very different circumstances.

All cemeteries have a free lot or town lot, an area set aside for the burial of those without the means to provide their own lot. In Old Parish Cemetery, this spot is located in the center of the burial ground at the base of a grassy slope. Research into those interred there revealed the poignant story of a family in distress.

The tale begins in 1890, when the Katzenmeier family—Margaret Katzenmeier and her sons, Charles, George, Henry and William—resided on Railroad Avenue. Charles and George worked at the New York and New England Railroad car shops on Lenox Street, Henry was a farmhand and William worked at the Winslow tannery. Soon enough, the family's troubles began. In 1890, the Town of Norwood paid for room, board and nursing services for Willie Katzenmeier; such payments were listed in the annual town report under the heading "Support for the Poor." In January 1891, Willie died of septicemia; he was twenty-two years old and was buried in the town lot. On December 27, 1895, George Katzenmeier, thirty-four, died suddenly of heart disease. The local newspaper reported that he was single, had many friends who mourned his loss and had worked in the boiler department at the car shops. The paper also wrote that he was of German descent and was buried beside his brother William in the old cemetery.

Meanwhile, Charles Katzenmeier was working as a house painter. By the end of 1895, however, Charles's name also appeared under "Support for the Poor" in the town's annual report, as the town paid for his board at the State Lunatic Hospital at Taunton. Founded in 1854 and later known as the Taunton State Hospital, the facility was the second such state asylum opened in Massachusetts. Despite the efforts and good intentions of staff, it was a foreboding place. Charles Katzenmeier died in 1898 at the hospital and was buried in the town lot alongside his brothers. The brothers' mother, Margaret, died in 1903; she, too, was interred in the old cemetery.

As the twentieth century dawned, interments in Old Parish Cemetery became infrequent. Between 1900 and 1910, there were, on average, only two burials there each year. During three of those years, there was one sole burial; one year, there were none. This, at a time when an average of just under one hundred deaths occurred in Norwood annually. As might be anticipated, those who were buried in the old graveyard continued to have connections to the community's past.

In 1908, William Ellis, who was "a much-esteemed old resident" of Norwood, died at his home on Nahatan Street. Born in 1830, he had married Anna Mariann Hurd in 1869 and had three children: Willie, Charles and Eva Mabel. William Ellis worked as a moulder at the J.F. Plimpton Foundry on Hill Street for his entire career. A private man who held no official position, Ellis was recalled, in an affectionate obituary in the *Norwood Messenger* on October 10, as "a hard-working, quiet, faithful man who had the good will of friends and neighbors. He was a man of great kindness of heart and probably had not an enemy in the world." In failing health for some time, he was reported to have "rallied considerably" during the summer, although it was acknowledged that he had not "regained his old strength." Shortly before he died, he visited an old friend who was also in poor health, and the two "had joked together about a planned hunting trip." William Ellis was seventy-eight when he passed away. He was survived by his widow, Anna, and daughter, Eva, both sons having predeceased their father.

A year later, on October 1, 1909, Norwood lost another link to its past when Charles Thompson, the son of Universalist minister Reverend Edwin Thompson, died suddenly. Born in East Walpole and educated in the Walpole public schools and at Dean Academy in Franklin, Thompson devoted much of his life to newspaper work, starting as the editor of the *Walpole Enterprise* early in his career. He subsequently traveled west and, for nine years, was associated with newspapers in and around Denver. Upon his return to Massachusetts, he was a correspondent for the *Boston Globe* and the Associated Press for several years. He then began work as a reporter and editorial writer for the *Norwood Advertiser and Review*, eventually writing and editing practically the entire newspaper.

For five years before his death, Thompson was a reporter for the *Norwood Messenger* and was also the Norwood correspondent for the *Dedham Transcript* and the *Dedham Standard*, using the pen name "Son Tom." He had a wide range of interests, gave lectures on several topics to local groups and organizations and became one of the best-known and most popular men in the community. Never married, Thompson boarded at the home of Robert Walsh and his family at 49 Maple Street. According to his colleagues, on the day of his death, Thompson had left the *Messenger*'s office in good spirits at 11:00 p.m. and headed home. He became ill a few hours later, and although his landlord immediately called for a physician, he lived for only an hour longer. A witty and pleasant conversationalist, Charles Thompson was greatly mourned by the staff at the *Messenger*, who assured their readers that he was "a good comrade, a loyal friend, and a talented writer." Charles Thompson was interred in the Thompson family lot beside his father, who had been an important figure in South Dedham in the mid-nineteenth century.

By the opening decades of the twentieth century, two large printing firms, Norwood Press and the Plimpton Press, had been added to Norwood's industrial base. At the same time, the Winslow Brothers and Smith tanneries and the Morrill Ink Works continued to thrive, as did a number of smaller commercial firms. This combination attracted immigrants from across Europe. As the area's population climbed from approximately eight thousand in 1910 to more than twelve thousand in 1920, so did the number of deaths that occurred there. Between 1911 and 1920, there were over 1,400 deaths recorded in Norwood; only eighteen bodies were buried in the old cemetery. Even a worldwide epidemic did not slow the cemetery's decline into obsolescence.

In 1918, an especially virulent pandemic of influenza spanned the globe, killing more than thirty million people in less than a year. On the local level, Norwood was devastated by the disease: thousands of residents were sickened, and well over one hundred succumbed. There were close to 250 burials in Norwood that year, almost double the usual number. And yet, even with such a substantial loss of life, only one of the victims of the epidemic was buried in Old Parish Cemetery. Edna McElhenney Reynolds, thirty-one, died of influenza on October 1, 1918. The daughter of Mr. and Mrs. Robert C. McElhenney, she had grown up in town and had been the chief operator at the Norwood Telephone Exchange for several years prior to her 1913 marriage to Lewis Reynolds. Making her death especially tragic, Edna had given birth to a daughter only a few days prior to her death. She was interred in the family lot beside her father, who had passed away in April 1918 of tuberculosis.

For the most part, the town and its people had turned away from the old burying ground. Automobiles and trolley cars traveled past the cemetery on Washington Street, by then a road that had been widened, paved and lined with two- and three-story brick commercial buildings. As Norwood modernized, the cemetery became a rarely thought of and easily overlooked remnant of a distant history. Ignored and neglected, it was little more than a macabre reminder of centuries past. "I used to like to

After Highland Cemetery was established, this older cemetery became obsolete and neglected. *OPPV Collection*.

wander around in a weedy old tumbledown New England graveyard that was directly in back of our house on Washington Street," one neighbor recalled later. "The weeds were waist-high, and you could lie down and hide in them. You could hide in them and speculate on the rows upon rows of skeletons lying on their backs in the dirt down below."[19]

8

NEGLECT

The twentieth century was not kind to Old Parish Cemetery. Throughout the 1920s and 1930s, burials dwindled, and many of those interred there were the last members of the old South Dedham families. Walter Dean Chickering passed away in 1923. The son of John Dean Chickering and the grandson of Mary Dean Chickering, Walter was born in 1857 in the Chickering house on Walpole Street and died there sixty-six years later. His mother, Amelia, had died at a young age, and his grandmother Mary Dean Chickering had raised him. The boy and grandmother became fast friends, with Mary Chickering telling the child stories of South Dedham's early history. Walter also recalled that as he walked to the village school as a boy, he passed only three houses: one belonging to Lewis Guild (the site of today's First Congregational Church), one belonging to Mark Hoyle (later the site of the Lewis Plimpton mansion, across from today's library) and the original church parsonage near the corner of Beacon and Walpole Streets. At the time of his death, Chickering was a janitor at the Masonic Temple. Having never married, he was the last of that family line.

Similarly, Nancy Maria Chamberlain was born in 1838 to two longtime Tiot village families. Her father, Isaac Chamberlain, and her mother, Nancy Morse Chamberlain, were buried in Old Parish as well. Nancy was educated by J. Nelson Stevens in South Dedham and attended a private school in Lawrence, Massachusetts. She was a schoolteacher in the Everett School in 1855 and 1856. She lived with her father and brother until her marriage to John B. Page in 1875, after which she kept house for her husband and his father for some twenty years. Following her husband's death, Nancy continued to live in their home at 397 Washington Street, eventually renting out rooms to boarders. Around midnight on the night of January 11, 1924, Page's boarder heard screams for help. When she ran to Page's rooms, she discovered her enveloped in flames. Despite the assistance of passersby who heard the commotion and the immediate response of fire personnel, Nancy Chamberlain Page was pronounced dead at the scene. It was believed that she had been sitting up late, reading—as was her custom—and she somehow tipped over a lamp, causing her clothing to ignite.

Another death that occurred in 1924 was that of Anna Pratt, who had been born in 1858 to another family of long-standing in South Dedham. Annie, as she was called, married Charles Walter Gould, a farmer, in 1878 and had one child, Stanley Curtis Gould. Sometime prior to 1900, Annie divorced Gould, and on July 11, 1900, Annie Pratt Gould, then a dressmaker, was married to Henry Arthur Smith, a carpenter. The couple lived at 165 Vernon Street in Norwood. Henry Smith died in June 1917. For a few years, Annie Smith and her son, Stanley Gould, who was a pressman either at Norwood Press or Plimpton Press, continued to reside in town. Around 1922, mother and son moved to Glendora, California, where Stanley continued to work as a pressman. On May 30, 1924, Annie was coming home to visit her brother Charles Pratt of Dedham when she was found unconscious in her berth on the train when it arrived in Boston. She was pronounced dead, and her passing was attributed to heart failure. She was buried beside her parents, Simeon and Charlotte Pratt.

Indicative of a diversifying town, however, some of those interred had more tenuous connections to old Tiot Village. Charles V. Bailey, a carpet printer, was born in 1823 in Maine and married Julia Ann Litchfield there. By 1870, Charles and Julia, along with their children, were living in South Dedham. Julia Ann Bailey died in October 1871 and was interred in Old Parish Cemetery. Two years later, Charles Bailey was married to Mary Elizabeth Burke Trask. By 1888, the family was living on Nahatan Street. Charles and Mary had a son, George Bailey, who was born in November 1878 and died in April 1899. Fred Bailey, the son of Charles and Julia Bailey, passed away in 1896 in his Norwood home after battling an illness for three weeks. He had been employed in the carpenter's shop at the railroad car shops, was very popular among his fellow employees and was mourned by a large circle of friends. Charles Bailey died in 1903, and Mary died in 1926. Both were interred in the family lot in Old Parish.

The gravestone of Annie Pratt Smith and her parents, Simeon and Charlotte Pratt, stands in the shade of a lovely mature oak. *OPPV Collection.*

Frank Bailey, the son of Charles and Julia, was an iron moulder. At various times, he lived on Hill Street, Nahatan Street and, in 1918, Walnut Avenue. Frank died in July 1921. He, too, was buried in the family plot along with his wife, Lizzie, who lived until the age of eighty-eight, when she died in May 1947. Beside their remains are those of their son Edward, who survived only one year; he was born in January 1883 and died in May 1884.

Born in Nova Scotia in 1832, David H. Corbett was in the United States by the early 1850s. He married Sarah P. McIntosh of Stoughton in 1856 and came to South Dedham shortly thereafter. Corbett was a blacksmith by trade. He worked for Charles Morse for five years, and then he hired J.W. Roby's shop and opened his own business with his brother Thomas. He stepped away from blacksmithing for a time because of a cancer diagnosis, but after his recovery, he was employed at the New York and New England car shops on Lenox Street until his death from pneumonia at the age of sixty-five in 1897. Corbett was an expert workman, was well regarded by Norwood residents and had many friends at the car shops.

Eighteen years later, in February 1915, Corbett's widow, Sarah P. McIntosh Corbett, seventy-six, died after a month-long illness. She, too, had a large circle of acquaintances and was a member of the Women's Relief Corps. Interred with the couple's remains were those of an infant son who had died in 1868; their son Herbert A. Corbett, who had predeceased his mother in 1903; and, finally, their daughter Sarah C. Corbett, who passed in 1935. The Corbett memorial is a twentieth-century polished granite stone with the tools of the blacksmith trade engraved on its face.

Marshall E. Brooks was born in 1847 in Nova Scotia, Canada, and immigrated to the United States with his wife, Amelia S. Angus Brooks. They had several children, including Frank and Ella May, who died at young ages of tuberculosis. Their daughter Violet appears to be their only child who reached adulthood. While living in South Dedham and, later, Norwood, Brooks was employed as a wheelwright, making or repairing wooden wheels. He likely found work at a local carriage shop or at the railroad car shops. Amelia Brooks died in 1876 of tuberculosis at the age of twenty-four.

In 1880, Marshall Brooks married Isabel Ross. Their daughter Marion was only two years old when she died in 1889. Marshall Brooks became a U.S. citizen in 1887 and, beginning in 1900, was a piano manufacturer in Boston. Isabel Brooks died in 1922. Twice a widower, Marshall Brooks retired and moved to Chapel Hill, North Carolina, to be with his son, who

The southern slope of Old Parish. The Corbett stone with its blacksmith's anvil stands in the foreground. *Courtesy of Halvorson | Tighe and Bond Studio.*

was a professor of sociology in Chapel Hill. Marshall Brooks died in 1927. Interred in Old Parish Cemetery are the remains of Marshall E. Brooks, both his wives and three of his children: Frank, Ella May and Marion.

Two years later, the death of Charles Adrian Bishop occurred under unusually modern circumstances. Born in 1859, Bishop arrived in South Dedham to work at the tannery and live with his aunt Sarah A. Webster. In 1885, he married Julia Ellen Godfrey, also a newcomer to town. The Bishops began their married life at 29 Hill Street and had four children: Frank E., who was born in 1887 and died at the age of three in 1890; Charles, born in 1890; Sidney, born in 1891; and an infant Bishop who was born and died in 1893. Through the years, Charles held various occupations, including working as a lamplighter, gas piper and ink mill worker. As the 1920s began, Bishop was employed as a steamfitter at the Lewis Manufacturing Company in Walpole. After his wife's death, Charles Bishop boarded with a family at 413 Washington Street in Norwood.

According to the *Norwood Messenger*, on Monday, September 30, 1929, Charles Bishop was crossing Washington Street near his home when he was struck by a car. He was rushed to Norwood Hospital with a compound fracture of his right leg, a possible skull fracture, contusions and abrasions. He was placed on the danger list and died early Tuesday morning. The driver of the vehicle, a Walpole resident, explained to the police that he had noticed a man in the road and had pulled to one side to pass him when, suddenly, his front fender struck Bishop. Charles Bishop was buried at Old Parish Cemetery alongside his aunt Sarah A. Webster and his son Frank E. Bishop.

By the time of Charles Bishop's fatal accident, burials were becoming ever more infrequent in the old cemetery. But a disturbing trend had emerged. Set back as it was from the street, unfenced and encircled by private property, the isolated graveyard was attracting unwelcome visitors. It had become a common shortcut for residents who were walking from Hill Street and beyond to get to Washington Street and downtown. People did not see the harm in that. However, the cemetery was also drawing the attention of loiterers and those bent on malicious mischief. The situation became serious enough that in 1929, the town's cemetery department highlighted the problem in its annual report. At least twelve gravestones had been pushed off their foundations during the year, including the memorials of John and Nancy Chamberlain Page, Joel Guild and the four stones belonging to the James Engles family, all on the northern side of the property. Some normal deterioration and weather damage was expected in a burial ground this old, but these toppled stones and the serious breaks to other monuments were obviously done by human hands. A year later, as the vandalism continued, the department recommended that an iron fence be erected around the entire cemetery—a futile request, as the town, like the rest of America, was facing the Great Depression.

In 1935, newspaperman Win Everett, whose own ancestors were interred in Old Parish, took note of the cracked and sagging stone doors on the tombs near Washington Street. He suggested that the restoration of these doors and their iron hinges might be a worthwhile project for federal monies. The previous year, Everett had secured funding from the Massachusetts Division of the Federal Emergency Relief Administration (FERA) to gather historical and genealogical data. There were actually two federal job-creating agencies that preceded the well-known Works Progress Administration (WPA) of the 1930s. One was FERA, and the other was the Civil Works Administration (CWA). Norwood had already benefited from a CWA program aimed at public buildings and grounds, including schools, libraries and road construction. Although federal money was eventually secured for certain improvements and the design and construction of an administration building at Highland Cemetery, no funding was forthcoming for an Old Parish project.

A year later, the death and burial of Willard Dean marked the end of a branch of the Dean family tree. Born in South Dedham on July 17, 1854, Willard Dean was the fourth generation to be born in the Dean homestead at the corner of Pleasant and Dean Streets. Built on land that had originally been a king's grant parcel, the house was one of the first in this section of Tiot Village. It was said that few alterations were made to the one-and-a-half-story house over some two hundred years of family life. While the surrounding property was open land when the house was built, by the end of Dean's lifetime, the area had become well populated, and the buildings of the Morrill Ink Works were within sight of the home.

A farmer, musician and great marksman with a rifle, Willard Dean was left a widower in 1887, when his wife, Frances, whose maiden name was also Dean, died at the age of thirty-nine of dysentery. Willard never remarried but continued to reside in his home alone for nearly fifty years until his death in February 1936. At the age of ninety-two, he was one of the oldest residents of the town at the time of his passing, and he left no surviving near relatives.

On September 16, 1937, a *Norwood Messenger* headline told the story: "Vandalism Ruins Old Cemetery." Frustrated by the multiple incidents

The stones of John Talbot and James Crooker (*left*) were toppled by human hands; those of Benjamin and Rene Dean (*right*) were felled by erosion. *OPPV Collection.*

of damage and disrespect at the burial ground, galvanized by what they considered to be the "sorry situation in the old cemetery" and realizing it was the "last, priceless relic of Colonial times," members of the Norwood Historical Society, led by Win Everett, consulted cemetery superintendent George Smith. According to the newspaper, their discussions "brought to light a sordid story of public neglect and desecration which has been going on for a long time in the old burying ground." Smith confirmed that the secluded spot had become a popular "cross-cut" for neighborhood folks, but it was also a "nightly rendezvous for drinking and petting parties." In addition, there were "drunken brawls" and adolescents with BB guns using some of the portrait gravestones for target practice. Smith reiterated that a fence around the entire perimeter would help solve the problem. Despite the group's well-intentioned efforts and publicity, the situation remained unchanged.

Six years later, in July 1943, a middle-aged man was seen leaving the cemetery grounds at three o'clock in the morning. Later that day, town employees discovered seven overturned headstones. In addition, flags from the graves of veterans had been removed, torn and tossed to the ground. The vandal was never found. Although the desecration persisted, the small cemetery crew, charged with maintaining the ever-expanding Highland Cemetery as well, not only cleared and mowed the grounds of Old Parish but made repairs to broken tombs and stones whenever possible.

Historian Win Everett reiterated his concern, writing in part, "The Old Cemetery was practically abandoned as a town burying place in 1881 when Highland Cemetery was opened. Many bodies have been moved from the old to the new in the intervening years. The families which now have any personal interest in the Old Cemetery are few. Little by little it has been forgotten by the older people and ignored by the wave of strangers who have engulfed the town." Everett was not wrong about the number of new residents who called Norwood home following World War II and into the 1950s. Although the large factories that had been the bedrock of Norwood's economy began to disappear, the construction of a modern highway system, coupled with postwar prosperity, brought about renewed industrial development and a housing boom. Soon, entire neighborhoods were being constructed, and Norwood became a bustling suburb.

Everett made particular reference to the fact that the once residential area around the cemetery had transitioned to commercial use. It had begun as early as the 1850s, when the Smith tannery plant, Fales's grain mill and several small foundries were situated to the east of the burial ground, beside the railroad tracks. The evolution continued into the twentieth century, as business establishments were built or residential properties were repurposed until, as the mid-twentieth century arrived, Old Parish was almost invisible behind a row of commercial structures.

After three years without an interment, in May 1947, Lizzie Bailey was brought to the lot in Old Parish that had been in her husband's family since 1871. That same year, a group of schoolchildren notified their teachers and the police of a cave-in of a tomb on the eastern side of the cemetery. Police Chief Thomas Lyon assured the public that no vandalism or desecration had occurred. The collapse of the ancient Sumner tomb was probably caused by an especially heavy rain and snow event that had occurred the previous weekend. Norwood's public works and cemetery departments repaired the damage as best they could.

Two years later, in July 1949, however, vandals again entered the graveyard and knocked over four large memorials. The size of the stones involved led officials to believe it was not the work of mischievous youths but malicious felons. The perpetrators also stole the bronze plaques from a handful of veterans' graves. This desecration of the graves of men who had served the country was especially disturbing to all.

The last two interments at Old Parish Cemetery took place in 1951 and 1960. Both had relevance to old Tiot and to the unique challenges faced by women in the modern age. In 1951, there were 181 burials in Norwood, and only one occurred at Old Parish Cemetery. Once again, the Bailey lot was the site of the interment. Ella Maria Trask Blackler was born in 1867 in Beverly, Massachusetts. Her parents were Charles Trask, a brick maker, and Mary Elizabeth Burke Trask. What happened to Charles Trask is uncertain, but Mary E. Burke Trask, thirty-five, married Charles Bailey in 1873 in Dedham. Bailey was forty-eight, and this was his second marriage. In 1880, Charles; his wife, Mary; a daughter, Ella Trask; and a son, George Bailey, were residing in Norwood.

On March 5, 1885, Ella Trask, eighteen, married John Blackler, a twenty-three-year-old shoe factory worker in Lynn, Massachusetts. They remained in Lynn for at least fifteen years. By 1910, however, Ella and John Blackler were living in Hannibal, Missouri, where John was a shoemaker. Ella Trask Blackler, a widow, returned to Norwood around 1920 and became a live-in servant/housekeeper in the Washington Street household of George and Louisa Lepper. Lepper owned the Norwood Garage, an automobile repair business. Ella Trask Blackler died alone in a nursing home at the age of eighty-three. She was interred in Old Parish Cemetery in February 1951 beside her mother, her stepfather and several of his children and their families.

In March 1960, the final recorded burial in Old Parish Cemetery took place. Born in September 1877 in Norwood, Eva Mabel Ellis was the daughter of Anna Mariann Hurd Ellis and William Ellis, an iron moulder. Eva grew up in Norwood and lived her early adult years with her parents while working as a book compositor at one of the town's mammoth book publishing firms. After her father's death in 1908, Eva continued to live with her mother at the family home on Nahatan Street and, later, in an apartment in the new Talbot building at the corner of Washington and Guild Streets. Erected in 1912, the Talbot building was the first commercial apartment building to be constructed in Norwood.

On November 12, 1919, Eva Mabel Ellis, forty-two, married Eugene Louis Richard in Boston. Richard worked on the railroad, lived in Providence, Rhode Island, and had been married previously. In the 1920 U.S. census, they were recorded as living with Eugene's parents in Providence. It is unclear when Eva and Eugene divorced, but by 1940, Eva Richard, divorced, appears in the census as an unemployed lodger in a rooming house in Cambridge, Massachusetts. She died on March 5, 1960, in Dorchester, at the age of eighty-two and was interred in Norwood along with her parents and brother, Willie. Like Ella Trask Blackler, Eva Ellis Richard died alone. No stone marks the grave of either woman.

Prior to Eva Ellis Richard's death, in 1958, another wave of cemetery desecration occurred. Thirty-two stones were pushed from their bases at Highland Cemetery; it was believed that an automobile must have been used in order to perpetrate such damage. Around the same time, fifteen stones were similarly damaged in the old cemetery. Some of these were repaired and reset on site; others were so badly broken that they were deemed irreparable and were brought to Highland Cemetery for storage.

In 1961, Norwood's Veterans' Council, which had been decorating graves in Old Parish, asked permission from town officials to erect a memorial for all the veterans interred at the old cemetery. Due to the vandalism the site had suffered over the years, the selectmen expressed their reluctance, mentioning once again the need for a fence. Eventually, they relented, however, and a stone marker was placed near the Washington Street entrance. Its bronze plaque reads: "Dedicated to the / veterans of the Colonial Wars, / Buried in this cemetery / Revolutionary War / War of 1812 / Civil War."

The cemetery department continued to maintain the grass, trees and shrubbery at Old Parish but were frustrated by the occasional deliberate toppling of monuments. This remained a significant problem until 1964, when, tragically, an adolescent was found in the cemetery, the victim of an accidental hanging. Within months, a chain link fence was installed around the entire perimeter. "This has completely stopped the loitering and vandalism," the cemetery superintendent's report stated. The move also closed the site to visitors. "If any one should want to visit into Old Parish Cemetery," he concluded, "they should call the Superintendent [of cemeteries] and arrange to have it opened for them."[20] Although the department continued to carry out routine maintenance in Old Parish, no further improvements were made. Still, from this point forward, the cemetery generally looked cared for despite its dormancy as a burial ground.

Two decades later, the cemetery was unequivocally encased. A large three-story office building was erected in 1984 on the north side of the graveyard. It joined a row of mixed-use housing and commercial buildings to the south. On the west, a brick professional building facing Washington Street had been erected in 1959, obscuring the burial ground from passing traffic. And to the east there was a parking lot and commuter rail stop. In addition, the cemetery's aging chain link fence had been breached in several places. It was perhaps no surprise, then, when serious vandalism and desecration

Badly damaged by vandals, fragments of the David Andrews family's memorial await restoration. *OPPV Collection*.

Erected in the 1960s, this monument honors the eighteenth- and nineteenth-century veterans buried in the cemetery. *OPPV Collection*.

began anew. In June 1984, in an act called "grotesque" by then–cemetery superintendent Paul Wollenhaupt, two of the tombs near the Washington Street entrance were broken into, coffins removed and pried open and bones taken. Admitting that the secluded site was once again the scene of underage drinking and instances of petty vandalism, Wollenhaupt could not recall a previous instance of such desecration. The coffins were returned to their tombs, and the doors were welded shut. Officials demanded better surveillance and security.

Six weeks later, in August 1984, another disconcerting incident occurred. Although no memorials were physically damaged, more than a dozen were disfigured by occult symbols and slogans spray painted in red. Not wanting to further damage the delicate, unpolished marble surfaces, cemetery workers covered the markings with white paint. Surveillance and lighting were increased. In May 1985, two Norwood residents were arraigned on charges stemming from this incident.[21]

For the next quarter of a century, the Old Parish Cemetery remained dormant and chiefly forgotten. Town employees kept the grass mown and cleared the leaves in the fall. In May each year, in anticipation of Decoration Day, later called Memorial Day, flowers were placed on the graves of some forty-nine veterans of early wars, a ritual started in the 1860s by surviving Civil War soldiers. In 1905, for the first time, the few remaining Civil War veterans were too old and frail to visit the cemetery, and the duty was passed on to members of the Sons of Veterans. Soon enough, they, too, were forced to give up the task. By the end of the twentieth century, it was cemetery workers, in conjunction with the veterans' agent, who placed those floral remembrances in this ancient burial ground. On Memorial Day itself, officials still gather here for a brief ceremony before the annual parade, which follows a route through the town and up to Highland Cemetery.

Few among the general public took note or were even aware of the gesture. As one writer put it, "The tombs, the fence, the granite posts of the gate and the road into the cemetery are all there today for those who want to see them. But few people in Norwood ever give this spot a kind look or a thought." For the most part, silence reigned among the slate and stone and sepulcher of Old Parish, a stillness broken only by the occasional historical tour or Halloween-themed program. It was not until 2018, more than two and a half centuries after the founding of the graveyard, that volunteers banded together to restore this sacred space and reassert its significance to a twenty-first century community.

9

PRESERVATION

I n some respects, a tour led by Veterans' Services director Ted Mulvehill in the spring of 2003 was the beginning of the ongoing effort to preserve Old Parish Cemetery. A bus brought passengers to seven sites around Norwood, including parks, cemeteries (both Highland and Old Parish), the town common and the municipal building, each of which hold significant memorials to veterans. By far the most popular stop was Old Parish Cemetery. While climbing its hill in a driving rain, participants— many of whom had never been inside the cemetery's fence—were awed by its physical landscape and historical significance. The tour was repeated six years later with the same response, and it became clear that with attention and imaginative programming, Old Parish could become a vibrant cultural resource to a community that had virtually forgotten about its existence.

With the cooperation of the cemetery department, the local historical society began to offer tours that highlighted the early veterans and their place in eighteenth- and nineteenth-century history. But it took a few more years for this interest to coalesce into an organization dedicated to the restoration and preservation of the site. As plans and a website were readied, permissions were acquired from town officials and nonprofit incorporation papers were assembled, the concept of the Old Parish Preservation Volunteers (OPPV) began to take root in the community. Well over four dozen attended a tour in the fall of 2017, and in April 2018, more than fifty came to OPPV's inaugural event, an illustrated talk by Rob Gregg, president of the Vine Lake Preservation Trust in Medfield, Massachusetts. (It was a lecture given by Gregg in 2015 that inspired the formation of OPPV.) As he outlined the trust's initiatives in preserving, enhancing, interpreting and celebrating Vine Lake Cemetery, the feasibility of doing the same in Old Parish Cemetery gathered support. Less than a month later, OPPV's first work session—two hours on a Saturday morning—drew close to forty men and women who were eager to learn about cemetery preservation.

In the ensuing weeks, Rob Gregg demonstrated the best techniques for cleaning, resetting and repairing gravestones. While cleaning is simple and requires only water, a harmless water-soluble solution and soft brushes, resetting is a slower process. Teams of two or three work together on a given stone; even more help may be needed if the monument is especially large or broken below ground. The repair of the stones, whether split by natural causes or broken by vandals, is a more complicated procedure that depends on the severity of the damage and the material itself. Once again, experienced workers taught the proper and appropriate use of lime mortar, two-part epoxy, stakes, clamps and other supplies and tools.

When he first walked through Old Parish, Gregg remarked that it was "a flashback" to the early days at Vine Lake, when he had seen "many broken memorials, tilting and leaning ones, memorials almost buried on their backs or fronts." And he continued, "I couldn't help but wonder how many gravestones you will discover which are completely hidden below grade." There were many.

The top half of the gravestone belonging to Newell Fisher was found right in front of the stone's base; it had been broken off and completely covered by grass. Newell Fisher was born in February 1803 in Dedham. His father was Oliver Fisher and his mother was Olive Smith Fisher. Both were buried in Old Parish. Newell Fisher married Betsey Farrington in 1825. Her parents, David Farrington and Susanna Fales Farrington, are interred nearby. The Fishers owned a farm and had three children: Lucy, Jason and George. We know little more about their lives. Betsey Farrington Fisher died in August 1875 of cholera at the age of seventy. A year later, the widowed Newell Fisher passed away. In the fall of 2021, the base of his monument was leveled, and the gravestone was mended and cleaned by volunteers.

The bottom section of the memorial to Elenor Ellis Fuller was revealed when sod was peeled back in the spring of 2020. Elenor Ellis of South Dedham had married Eliphalet Fuller in 1786. In August 1827, according to records, "while in perfect health, Eliphalet Fuller dropped down dead in his field at work." There is no record of where he was buried. Elenor Ellis Fuller died in 1844; she was eighty-six years old. Her son Ellis, who served

Volunteers work to straighten and reset a tilting two-hundred-year-old gravestone.
OPPV Collection.

on the Dedham Board of Selectmen for seven years beginning in 1833, passed away in 1857. Ellis; his wife, Lucy Gay Fuller, who died in 1868; and his brother Ira were all buried in the family lot.

Once the bottom half of the stone had been uncovered, the top of Elenor Fuller's stone was found at Highland Cemetery, where it had been stored along with several other damaged memorials awaiting restoration to their original grave sites. Later in the spring of 2020, OPPV reunited the two halves and reset the stone. It now stands, whole and upright, for the first time in decades. Other memorials in the family lot still require some repair.

At the peak of the graveyard's hill, entire rows of slate headstones were sagging, sunken or leaning on one another. These were realigned and reset. In doing so, the OOPV found accompanying footstones. In the eighteenth century, a headstone was placed at the head of the grave to identify the person who was buried there. An inscription usually contained a person's name, dates of birth and death and perhaps an epigraph. But graves also often had a footstone, a small marker used to delineate the length of the grave, similar to a bed's headboard and footboard. Usually, the footstone was engraved with only a person's initials; occasionally, it would contain additional information. Apart from serving as a demarcation of the grave from head to foot, these markers prevented people from stepping on the grave, something considered disrespectful and an invitation of bad luck. Additionally, having both a headstone and a footstone helped avoid accidental excavation in an overcrowded graveyard. The tradition generally ceased during the nineteenth century. Several of these small stones had fallen over and were covered by grass near the appropriate memorial; others had likely been pulled up and strewn across the site decades earlier by mischievous trespassers. A few footstones, including those belonging to Reverend Thomas Balch and Captain William Bacon, were located at Highland Cemetery and returned to Old Parish to be set in place.

The satisfying process of resetting rows of colonial-era stones often brought lost inscriptions to light. Some, like that on the slate stone belonging to Lucy Gay, remain poignant, even now. Lucy was one of three sisters who died between 1779 and 1793, and her stone reads, "In Memory of Lucy / Daugh'r of Cap't Jesse / & Mrs. Sarah Gay, / who died April 3rd, / 1791, aged 17 / years wanting 9. / Days." It is the only stone found to date in the cemetery with an age written in that fashion. One can almost imagine the teenager looking forward to her seventeenth birthday.

Records of early deaths, compiled and transcribed in the 1880s, along with surveys of the lots and interments in the "old burying ground," were consolidated and expanded to include, whenever possible, the complete birth and death dates, the cause of death, an accurate transcription of inscriptions, the name of the stone carver and other distinctive details of these grave sites. Research of existing digitized records and newspapers, even microfilm reels, added significant information. This is an ongoing project, constantly updated with newly discovered material. Gravestone scholars Laurel Gabel

Left: This portion of the memorial of Elenor Ellis Fuller was unearthed in the spring of 2020. *OPPV Collection.*

Below: The headstones and corresponding footstones of colonial-era villagers are today reunited and reset thanks to volunteers. *OPPV Collection.*

and Vincent Luti, among others, are generous about sharing their expertise on stone cutters and other aspects of the graveyard.

Larger projects have presented themselves. The stone and base belonging to Joel Morse, who died in 1826, were separated. Volunteers found the base at the bottom of the cemetery's hill and the stone at the top. Joel Morse was born in 1785, one of ten children born to Seth Morse Jr. and Mary Dean Morse. Sometime in 1813, Joel Morse married Azubah Hodges, who was born in New Hampshire. They had two sons, Joel and Mark, both of whom moved away from South Dedham after they married. Joel Morse died "very suddenly, probably in a fit," in June 1826 at the age of forty-one. Azubah Hodges Morse died in 1850. Their stone and base were brought back together, and the memorial was reset next to the gravestones belonging to Joel's parents. Similarly, the large obelisk erected in memory of Peter Wagner, a German immigrant who drowned in 1862, was found on its side near the Washington Street entrance to the cemetery. It was returned to its original site and reset in 2022 (see the image on page 75).

There is no shortage of volunteers anxious to assist in the preservation of Old Parish. In the spring of 2019, the burial ground became the site of an Eagle Scout project. For several work sessions, Boy Scouts probed the lots of Ebenezer Fisher Talbot and the family of Ezra Morse, another son of Seth and Mary Dean Morse. Born in 1791, Ezra married Sally Baker of Dedham in 1815. They had seven children: Charles Edwin, Cynthia, Osborn, Sidney, Reuben, Howard and Alvin. At various times, Ezra worked as a farmer, yeoman and wheelwright to support his family. Sadly, Ezra and Sally outlived most of their own children. Reuben died of dysentery in 1828 at only three years of age. Osborn passed away in 1847; he was twenty-seven years old, single and a farmer when he drowned. Howard, who died at twenty-eight; Cynthia, who died at forty-three; and Alvin, who died at thirty-one, all died of tuberculosis between 1860 and 1867. None of them had married. Tuberculosis continued to plague the family when Sidney's wife died of the same disease in 1869.

Charles Edwin Morse, the couple's eldest son, was born in 1815. In 1840, he married Abigail Colburn, also of Dedham. They had two sons, Charles and Arthur. Abigail Morse died in 1854 of tuberculosis. In 1858, Charles married Harriet Wales Fletcher, a widow and former schoolteacher. A little more than a year later, in December 1859, Charles E. Morse, who worked as a wheelwright, died of tuberculosis, leaving his two sons, then thirteen and sixteen years of age, in Harriet's care. She provided for the two until they completed college. Harriet Morse later opened a private school at her home at 880 Washington Street in Norwood. Her school had an excellent reputation and remained open until 1905. When she passed away in 1907, she was considered the last of a generation of "old-time teachers." Charles, along with his two wives, was buried in this family lot. Only Sidney outlived his parents. Ezra Morse died on January 27, 1873, of pleurisy fever, and his wife, Sally Baker Morse, passed away three years later in 1880 of old age. Under the careful supervision of mentors and volunteers, Boy Scouts cleaned the large Talbot and Morse monuments. In addition, as they worked, they uncovered several small individual markers, repaired and reset them (see the image on page 81).

In the quest to preserve Old Parish Cemetery and to encourage townspeople to explore and enjoy this cultural resource, OPPV has sponsored a wide variety of programs and events. Tours are offered each fall with titles such as "Civil War Veterans," "The Women of Old Parish" and even "Murder and Mayhem," which focused on the more headline-driven side of village life. Since 2018, volunteers have staffed open hours on Memorial Day and Veterans Day for the community to drop by, ask questions, and walk through the cemetery. It is hoped that, with new fencing and lighting, the graveyard will once again be open to the public at all times.

A more ambitious program was first organized on July 4, 2019. Sponsored through a grant from the Massachusetts Cultural Council and Mass Humanities, a public reading of Frederick Douglass's July 5, 1852 speech, "What to the Slave Is the Fourth of July?" was held at the grave site of Unitarian minister and abolitionist Reverend Edwin Thompson, a

Frederick Douglass's 1852 speech is read by townspeople as part of Norwood's July Fourth calendar of events. *OPPV Collection.*

The gathering audience, the advertisement on the town common and a scene from the production of Thornton Wilder's *Our Town* held in the cemetery. *OPPV Collection.*

contemporary of Frederick Douglass. This event, which is free, has drawn over forty readers each year and an audience of more than one hundred and has already become a part of Independence Day events in Norwood.

In 2022, the town of Norwood celebrated its 150th anniversary. To commemorate that event and to thank the townspeople for their support and encouragement, OPPV sponsored a performance of Thornton Wilder's famed play *Our Town* in the graveyard. The "stage" was the open, even walkway on the northern side of the cemetery. The cast was made up of volunteers who spent six weeks in rehearsals to bring this drama free of charge to the community. The audience, with folding chairs and blankets, sat on the gentle slope, which formed a natural amphitheater in front of the stage. Those who recognized the stirring tones of Norwood's carillon bells, housed in the town hall tower within view and hearing range of the cemetery, were delighted that this unique instrument was incorporated into the performance. While the relevance of early twentieth-century small town life was entertaining, the final act, which takes place in a cemetery, was especially moving, as the cast and audience alike were surrounded by actual gravestones.

Several cast members in *Our Town* were students from Norwood High School's drama department; their teacher played a major role as well. The interest and willingness of these young people to participate is indicative of the townwide support the preservation project has generated. History students have visited the cemetery as part of local history curricula, participated in the Reading Frederick Douglass program and have volunteered for work sessions. In the fall of 2022, high school art classes toured the burial ground and then mounted a first-ever art installation within its grounds. *Coloring the Old Parish Landscape: Visual Interpretations of*

Norwood's Historical Data drew its inspiration from birth, death, business and immigration statistics, which were compiled, analyzed and represented in colorful displays constructed of weather-impervious cloth, yarn, metal and wood.

The landscape of Old Parish plays a vital role in another important part of OPPV's mission: the development of a master plan for the preservation of the cemetery. The plan was underwritten by Norwood's Community Preservation Fund. The Commonwealth of Massachusetts's Community Preservation Act (CPA) helps towns preserve historic sites and open space, create affordable housing and develop outdoor recreational facilities. Monies are raised locally through a surcharge on property taxes and an annual distribution administered by the State Department of Revenue. The Town of Norwood voted to enact the CPA in 2017. A committee oversees applications for projects and brings recommendations to town meetings, which have the final vote on any use of the funds.

The funding for the development of a master plan for Old Parish Cemetery was approved in 2020. A professional landscape architectural firm was chosen, and their assessment and recommendations were completed in 2021. As the study confirmed, the topography of the cemetery is its defining landscape feature. Unmarked by paved paths, the sloping lawn is complemented by a few mature oak, American elm, gray birch and eastern white pine trees. Recommendations were made about the maintenance of vegetation on steep slopes, planting improvements and landscape interventions to halt erosion. One significant need is the structural restoration of the Sumner and Bird tombs on the eastern side of the site. Nearly hidden from the occasional visitor, these two tombs that stand near the Railroad Avenue entrance to the cemetery have been badly damaged by erosion and the incursion of vegetation. They belong to two of the most prominent and influential families in the area.

Although there are no existing records regarding those interred in the Sumner tomb, it is highly likely it's the burial place of Nathanael Sumner and his wife, Hannah Bullard Sumner. Born in 1720, Nathanael Sumner was a 1739 graduate of Harvard College, where he studied theology. Although he never served as a minister, he became a deacon of the Second Parish in 1752, while Reverend Thomas Balch was still pastor. On the secular side, Sumner was a representative to the general court for several years between 1756 and 1770, a Dedham selectman for nineteen years and a delegate to the colonial convention held in Faneuil Hall in 1768. Although he was fifty-five years old at the time, Sumner responded to the militia alarm on April

19, 1775, ready to defend his home and village against British hostilities. Local historian Win Everett later deemed Nathanael Sumner to be Tiot's most prominent Revolutionary War figure.

Sumner and his wife, Hannah, had six children who grew to adulthood and prospered. The family owned a large farm on the southern end of Tiot, bordering on Walpole. Today's Sumner Street was named for the family. Sumner was a man of distinction and means and one of only a few men in the village who enslaved people. (Reverend Thomas Balch was another.) Although Sumner left no account of this, the parish record indicates that "Eunice, a baptized Negro, belonging to Nathanael Sumner," passed away on February 3, 1774. Where Eunice was buried is unknown.

Around 1826, a "new burying ground" was founded in the southernmost part of the village; later generations of the Sumner family were interred there. Nathanael and Hannah, however, died in 1802 and 1806, respectively, long before that graveyard was an option. Situated just inside the entrance from Cemetery Street, the tomb would have originally been in a most prominent position, but the destructive floods of the nineteenth century and subsequent erosion left the tomb in a state of disrepair. It was this tomb that collapsed in 1947 and was then hurriedly closed off by cemetery workers. It is in critical need of restoration.

A short distance away from this tomb stands the remnant of the George Bird family tomb. George Bird was born in Cushing, Maine, in 1770. At an early age, he came to Needham, Massachusetts, where he learned to make

The tombs of Nathanael Sumner and George Bird, both on the eastern side of the graveyard, are in need of considerable restoration. *Courtesy of Halvorson | Tighe and Bond Studio.*

paper by hand. He married Martha C. Newell of Dover in 1798, and the couple had eight children. For several years, Bird was the superintendent of a paper mill in Milton, but in 1803, he purchased his own mill on Mother Brook in East Dedham. In 1812, he moved the plant to East Walpole, where he first made paper for United States currency. He brought his son Josiah Newell Bird into the business and called it Bird and Son.

In 1838, a new partnership was formed among George Bird, his sons Francis and Josiah and his son-in-law Harrison G. Park. Park left the business in 1840, and in 1842, George and Josiah Bird stepped away from the firm, leaving the company in the hands of Francis W. Bird, who made a great success of the enterprise. Bird and Sons, as it was known for decades, expanded its product line from simply paper into roofing material, shingles and floor covering, and its physical plant spread from East Walpole into Norwood. It remained in the family until the company was purchased by CertainTeed in the late twentieth century.

George Bird died in 1854, two years after the death of his wife, Martha C. Newell Bird. His death was attributed to old age, and he was still identified as a paper maker. The couple is interred in the family's tomb in the parish cemetery. They were joined there by their son Josiah Newell Bird and his wife, Martha B. Dean Bird, whose parents, Ebenezer and Lois Morse Dean, are interred in Old Parish as well. Josiah Newell Bird died in 1866 of heart failure; Martha passed away in 1885 of cancer. Plaques to their memory were attached to the tomb's granite surround. Most of what must have been a handsome and substantial tomb has been lost, leaving only a bricked-up entrance, the tomb's door and these two memorial fragments. Once restored, the door and these memorials will be reinstalled. Other members of the Bird family, including Francis W. Bird and subsequent generations, are interred in the new burying ground, which was established in 1826 and is today known as the Charles Sumner Bird Memorial Cemetery.[22]

The four tombs belonging to the Morse, Guild, Chickering and Kingsbury families near the Washington Street entrance need extensive restoration as well (see the image on page 21). Although their granite surrounds and lintels have held, the doors are cracked, and the rusted wrought-iron hinges and clasps are in poor condition. Across the graveyard, other monuments need expert care. For example, the memorial to the David Andrews family was shattered by vandals; the bottom still stands, but the top is in ragged pieces, some of which remain missing (see the image on page 115).

David Andrews was born in 1773. He was the eldest child of David Andrews and Hannah Fuller Andrews.

On April 18, 1797, David Andrews married Susan Fisher, known as Susey, the daughter of Benjamin Fisher and Mary Robbins Fisher of Walpole. David and Susey owned a farm on Pleasant Street in South Dedham and were the parents of several children, including David, Mary, Caroline, Hannah, Hannah F., Mary R. and Joel. Tragically, three of their daughters died at young ages. Mary was only three years old when she passed away in 1804; Hannah was about the same age when she died in 1809. Later, Susey Andrews gave birth to two more daughters, Hannah F., born in 1810, and Mary R., born in 1816. Hannah F. grew to adulthood and married. Mary R. died in 1824 at the age of eight; her death was attributed to typhus fever.

Susey Fisher Andrews died in June 1841. The record of her death states that she was "the first person that was carried on the new hearse." Obviously, the South Church was pleased with the acquisition of a new bier to transport the coffin of their fellow parishioners to the cemetery. David Andrews died in 1858; he was eighty-five. Their daughter Caroline had passed away a few years earlier in September 1853 of liver disease at the age of fifty. Apparently, both David and Susey were devout Christians; each

The well-cared-for Old Parish Cemetery today is a solemn, contemplative space for an appreciative community. *OPPV Collection.*

has a distinctive epigraph on the family's memorial. An exceptionally tall monument, it is inscribed: "DAVID ANDREWS / Born April xx 1773, / Died Dec. 14, 1858. / His last wishes were, / 'Lord Jesus, receive my spirit.' / SUSAN F., / wife of David Andrews / Died June 30, 1841: / aged 64 yrs, 7mos. / Blessed are the dead who die in the Lord. / MARY. / Died Aug. 16, 1804: / aged 3 yrs. 6 mos. / HANNAH. / Died Aug 3, 1809: / aged 3 yrs. 10 mos. / MARY R. / Died Nov. 11, 1824: / aged 8 yrs. 10 mos. / Children of D & S.F. Andrews. / CAROLINE. / daughter of the same. / died Sept. 30, 1853, aged 50." Damage has rendered the actual date of David's birth indecipherable. In time, the stone will be repaired and preserved. It is one of many that need the attention of volunteers.

Old Parish Cemetery is the final resting place of close to one thousand former residents of the town of Norwood—or, for many of them, the village of South Dedham. It is a space that was set aside over 250 years ago by the men and women of the South Parish as a burying ground for their dead. In the ensuing years, decades and even centuries, as the town and the world have been transformed, this place has remained unchanged: two acres of uneven terrain and rolling lawn, dotted by gravestones, frozen in time. And yet, if one looks closely, Old Parish is much more. Filled with centuries-old artifacts, it is an outdoor museum prepared to impart historical, cultural and artistic lessons to those willing to listen. It is a peaceful, timeless place in a frenzied world—a space suited for those seeking solitude or contemplation. While resetting a gravestone, one of OPPV's volunteers put it best, "I come here and work to pay my respects. I hope a hundred years from now, someone's doing this for us. No one wants to just be forgotten."

NOTES

1. Origins

1. Unless otherwise specified, all quotations in this book that are attributed to the writings of W.W. "Win" Everett are from *Remembering Norwood*.
2. All quotations included in this book that are attributed to Francis O. Tinker are from Tinker, "History of Norwood."

2. Duty-Bound

3. "Old Home Day," *Norwood Advertiser and Review*, August 1, 1902, 1.

3. Artists in Stone

4. Endicott family correspondence, Canton (Massachusetts) Historical Society.

4. Crises and Change

5. Recollection of the death of Reverend Alfred Bassett by Reverend Edwin Thompson, undated newspaper clipping, Norwood Historical Society.

6. F. Holland Day Archives, undated notes on Old Parish Cemetery, Norwood Historical Society. The "dreadful storm that washed away part of the new railroad" occurred on January 22, 1855, according to a diary quoted by Win Everett in "I've Been Workin' on the Railroad," *Norwood Messenger* (hereafter *NM*), May 7, 1935, 1.
7. George Hill, *Souvenir Program—Dedication Exercises of the Norwood Press*, quoted in Franklin, *Norwood: Centennial History*, 11–12.
8. C.L. Edwards, "A Case of Hydrophobia," *Boston Medical and Surgical Journal* 96, no. 11 (March 15, 1877): 303–4; "Fatal Hydrophobia Case," *Boston Daily Globe*, February 17, 1877, 8; Philip M. Teigen, "Legislating Fear and the Public Health in Gilded Age Massachusetts," *Journal of the History of Medicine and Allied Science* 62, no. 2 (April 2007): 141–70.
9. "An Act to Provide for a Change of Grade of the Old Cemetery in Norwood," in *Laws and Resolves Passed by the Legislature of Massachusetts* (Boston: Commonwealth of Massachusetts, April 1, 1885), 65.

5. Abolition and Rebellion

10. Win Everett, "The Book Is Closed!" *NM*, May 28, 1935, 1.
11. Edwin Thompson, letter dated November 25, in "Reminiscences of Rev. Edwin Thompson, 1887," newspaper clipping, source unknown, reconstructed from Gould scrapbook, Walpole Historical Society, 29, 38, 39.
12. Win Everett, "Silhouettes of Old Tyot, Number 1," *NM*, March 31, 1936, 2.
13. Lucy Cutler Kellogg, *History of the Town of Bernardston, Massachusetts* (Bernardston, MA: Town of Bernardston, 1902), 167–68.
14. Thornton Wilder, *Our Town* (New York: Perennial Classics, 2003), 87.

6. Families and Community

15. Town of Norwood, *Annual Reports*, January 31, 1880–January 31, 1890; "Obituary. Benjamin D. Guild," *Norwood Advertiser & Review*, September 14, 1889, 1.
16. "One Hundred Years Old," *Norwood Advertiser & Review*, June 11, 1897, 4; "A Notable Birthday," *Norwood Advertiser & Review*, supplement, June 18, 1897, 1; "Norwood Locals," *Norwood Advertiser & Review*, July 30, 1897, 4.
17. "Aged Men See Newest Sport," *Boston Globe*, September 13, 1910, 8.

7. Obsolescence

18. "Taken for a Burglar, An Aged Veterinary Surgeon Shot and Killed," *Boston Globe*, June 19, 1882, 1; "The Shooting of Dr. Gay, George Edmunds Exonerated by the Trial Justice," *Boston Globe*, July 8, 1882, 2. The story was summarized by Win Everett in "Manslaughter on Buttermilk Plain" in *Remembering Norwood*.
19. Mitchell, *Gould's Secret*, 66.

8. Neglect

20. The death of the fourteen-year-old boy was reported in both the *Norwood Messenger* and *Boston Globe* in March 1964; Report of Cemetery Department, Town of Norwood Annual Report, year ending on December 31, 1964, 228.
21. Tom Bowman, "Gruesome Find at Norwood Cemetery," *Daily Transcript*, June 27, 1984, 1, 7; Tom Bowman, "Vandals Spray Paint Gravestones," *Daily Transcript*, August 13, 1984, 1, 8; "Two Arraigned for Cemetery Vandalism," *Daily Transcript*, May 7, 1985, 28.

9. Preservation

22. Although he lived close by, Charles Sumner Bird was not related to the Sumner family of South Dedham. He was named after the famed abolitionist Senator Charles Sumner of Massachusetts.

SELECTED BIBLIOGRAPHY

Blachowicz, James. *From Slate to Marble: Gravestone Carving Traditions in Eastern Massachusetts, 1770–1870*. Evanston, IL: Graver Press, 2006.

———. *From Slate to Marble: Gravestone Carving Traditions in Eastern Massachusetts, 1750–1850*. Vol. 2. Evanston, IL: Graver Press, 2015.

Chase, Theodore, and Laurel K. Gabel. *Gravestone Chronicles*. Boston: New England Historic Genealogical Society, 1990.

De Lue, Willard. *The Story of Walpole 1724–1924*. Norwood, MA: Ambrose Press, 1925.

Endicott letters. Canton Historical Society Archives (Canton, MA).

Everett, Win. *Remembering Norwood: Win Everett's Tales of Tyot*. Edited by Heather S. Cole and Edward J. Sweeney. Charleston, SC: The History Press, 2008.

"Extracts from the Diary and Note Book of Captain William Bacon—1756." The Dedication of a Monument to the Memory of the Men of Walpole and Vicinity who Served in the French and Indian War (November 2, 1901). Walpole Historical Society Collection.

Fanning, Patricia J. *Influenza and Inequality: One Town's Tragic Response to the Great Epidemic of 1918*. Amherst: University of Massachusetts Press, 2010.

———. *Keeping the Past: Norwood at 150*. Staunton, VA: American History Press, 2021.

———. *Norwood: A History*. Charleston, SC: Arcadia Publishing, 2002.

Fenn, Elizabeth A. *Pox Americana: The Great Smallpox Epidemic of 1775–1782*. New York: Hill and Wang, 2001.

Fischer, David Hackett. *Paul Revere's Ride*. New York: Oxford University Press, 1994.

Forbes, Harriette Merrifield. *Gravestones of Early New England and the Men Who Made Them, 1653–1800*. New York: Da Capo Press, 1967.

Hanson, Robert B. *Dedham 1635–1890*. Dedham, MA: Dedham Historical Society, 1976.

Hill, Don Gleason (town clerk), comp. *An Alphabetical Abstract of the Record of Deaths, in the Town of Dedham, Massachusetts, 1844–1890*. Dedham, MA: Office of the Dedham Transcript, 1895.

———. *Record of Baptisms, Marriages and Deaths, and Admissions to the Church and Dismissals Therefrom. Transcribed from the Church Records in the Town of Dedham, Massachusetts, 1638–1845*. Dedham, MA: Office of the Dedham Transcript, 1888.

Huntoon, Daniel T.V. *History of the Town of Canton, Norfolk County, Massachusetts*. Canton, MA: J. Wilson and Son, 1893.

Lewis, Isaac Newton. *A History of Walpole, Mass*. Walpole, MA: First Historical Society of Walpole, 1905.

Lockridge, Kenneth A. *A New England Town, the First Hundred Years*. New York: W.W. Norton and Company, 1985.

Luti, Vincent F. "Eighteenth-Century Gravestone Carvers of the Upper Narragansett Basin: The Real George Allen, Jr." *Markers* 27 (2011): 89–113.

———. *In Death Remember'd: 18th Century Gravestone Carvers of the Taunton River Basin Massachusetts*. Staunton, VA: American History Press, 2017.

McCullough, David. *1776*. New York: Simon and Schuster Paperbacks, 2005.

Mitchell, Joseph. *Joe Gould's Secret*. New York: Viking Press, 1965.

Schiff, Stacy. *The Revolutionary Samuel Adams*. New York: Little, Brown and Co., 2022.

Tinker, Francis. "History of Norwood, Massachusetts." In *History and Directory of Norwood, Massachusetts for 1890*. Boston: Press of Brown Bros., 1890.

Tolles, Bryant Franklin, Jr. *Norwood: The Centennial History of a Massachusetts Town*. Norwood, MA: Town of Norwood, 1973.

INDEX

ABOUT THE AUTHOR

Patricia J. Fanning is a lifelong resident of Norwood, Massachusetts, and professor emerita of sociology at Bridgewater State University. A former president of the Norwood Historical Society and current president of the Old Parish Preservation Volunteers, she has written several books related to the town of Norwood, including *Norwood: A History* (2002), *Images of America: South Norwood* (2004), *Influenza and Inequality: One Town's Tragic Response to the Great Epidemic of 1918* (2010) and *Keeping the Past: Norwood at 150* (2021).